CBT Worksheets for Anxiety

A SIMPLE CBT WORKBOOK TO RECORD YOUR PROGRESS
WHEN YOU USE CBT FOR ANXIETY

Dr James Manning & Dr Nicola Ridgeway

Published by the West Suffolk CBT Service Ltd

CBT Worksheets for Anxiety

About the authors

Dr Nicola Ridgeway is a Consultant Clinical Psychologist and an accredited cognitive and behavioural therapist. She lectured on cognitive behaviour therapy (CBT) at the University of East Anglia, Norfolk, England, and the University of Essex for many years before becoming the Clinical Director of the West Suffolk CBT Service Ltd. Together with Dr James Manning she has co-authored several books on CBT.

Dr James Manning is a Consultant Clinical Psychologist and the Managing Director of the West Suffolk CBT Service. James has post-graduate qualifications in both Clinical Psychology and Counselling Psychology. An award-winning author, he has regularly offered workshops and training to clinicians throughout the United Kingdom on cognitive behaviour therapy and continues to work as a therapist.

By the authors

A Journey with Panic*

CBT Worksheets

CBT Worksheets for Anxiety

CBT Worksheets for Teenage Social Anxiety

Fused: A memoir of childhood OCD and adult obsession**

How to Befriend, Tame, Manage and Teach Your Black Dog Called Depression Using CBT***

How to Help Your Loved One Overcome Depression

My CBT Journal

The Little Book on CBT for Depression

* Winner of the Beverley Hills Book Awards (2016); Huffington Post's best self-published works (2016); Indie Reader Discovery Awards winner (2016); Non Fiction Authors Association Award winner (2016).

**New England Book Festival winner (2017); Pacific Book Awards winner (2017); Book Readers Appreciation Group winner (2017).

***Shortlisted for the International Rubery Award (2017).

Contents

1 .... How to use this book

2 .... A summary of CBT for anxiety

2 .... Assessing your anxiety

5 .... What is CBT?

18 .... Observing yourself

24 .... Cognitive distortions

28 .... Rules

34 .... Beliefs

37 .... Drawing out CBT cycles

37 .... Beliefs, rules, and behaviour cycles

43 .... The traditional CBT cycle

45 .... The generic CBT cycle

49 .... Social anxiety cycles

53 .... Health anxiety cycles

57 .... OCD cycles

63 .... CBT cycles for panic attacks

69 .... Breaking cycles

73 .... Break anxiety cycles created by thoughts and images

76 .... Challenging NATs

95 .... Learning how to interact with feelings in a different way

96 .... A counter-intuitive solution to anxiety

100 .... Altering the body's physiological processes to break cycles of anxiety

108 .... Break anxiety cycles by changing behaviour

115 .... Potential behavioural experiments for social anxiety

117 .... Potential behavioural experiments for anxiety and panic attacks

118 ....Potential behavioural experiments for health anxiety

119 ....Potential behavioural experiments for OCD

120 .... Potential behavioural experiments for phobic anxiety

128 .... Conclusion

133 ....References and additional reading

135 .... Medication

137 .... Glossary

138 .... Index

Tables

20 .... Table 1. Example of Situation, thought, emotion, and behaviour sheet

21 .... Table 2. A situation, thought, emotion, and behaviour sheet

32 .... Table 3. Rule challenging exercise

78 .... Table 4. Ben's NAT challenging record

81 .... Table 5. Alice's thought challenging record

96 .... Table 6. A new approach to feelings

104 .... Table 7a. Safe place exercise

105 .... Table 7b. Safe place exercise

111 .... Table 8. Jenny's list

113 .... Table 9. Jenny's behavioural experiments

123 .... Table 10. Example of a systematic desensitisation sheet

124 .... Table 11. Example of a systematic desensitisation sheet

126 .... Table 12. Jenny's exposure sheet

131 .... Table 13. An example of the law of opposites

Figures

6 ....Figure 1. Basic brain organisation

7 ....Figure 2. Location of the amygdala

9 ....Figure 3. How worry keeps itself going

12 ....Figure 4. Negative reinforcement

12 ....Figure 5. An advanced example of negative reinforcement in action

35 ....Figure 6. An example of a downward arrow exercise

37 ....Figure 7. An example of a connection between beliefs, rules, and behaviours

38 .... Figure 8. A more developed example

40 ....Figure 9. Jane's cycle of beliefs, rules, and behaviours

41 ....Figure 10. Nicola's cycle of beliefs, rules, and behaviours

43 ....Figure 11. An example of a traditional CBT cycle

46 .... Figure 12. Vera's generic CBT cycle

47 .... Figure 13. Gerry's CBT cycle

50 ....Figure 14. An example of social anxiety

51 .... Figure 15. A model of social anxiety (adapted)

54 ....Figure 16. Jenny's belief, rules, and behaviour cycle

55 .... Figure 17. Jenny's health anxiety cycle

58 ....Figure 18. Peter's beliefs, rules, and behaviour cycle

59 .... Figure 19. Peter's OCD cycle

60 ....Figure 20. An alternative OCD cycle

64 ....Figure 21. Example of a beliefs, rules, and behaviours cycle for panic

65 ....Figure 22. Example of a cycle for panic

67 .... Figure 23. Example of a self-phobic response

70 ....Figure 24. Breaking an anxiety cycle from several different angles

71 ....Figure 25. An example of a completed goal sheet

73 ....Figure 26. Intensity of emotion connected to thoughts

77 ....Figure 27. Ben's NAT placed in an adapted social anxiety CBT cycle

79 .... Figure 28. Ben's positive CBT cycle

80 .... Figure 29. Alice's panic cycle

82 .... Figure 30. Alice's new positive cycle

94 ....Figure 31. Gregory's example

96 ....Figure 32. Behaviours that maintain anxiety

How to use this book

An important part of cognitive behaviour therapy (CBT) is making records. Whether you are completing CBT on your own, CBT online, or CBT with the help of a therapist, this book can be used to assist you with your progress. This book can also act as a memory aid and to complement CBT homework tasks.

This book contains several blank worksheets, which you are very welcome to photocopy. Alternatively, you can purchase the diary that accompanies this book, called *CBT Diary & Worksheets*. It contains blank worksheets only, so that you can keep your worksheets together in one place.

CHAPTER 1

A summary of CBT for anxiety

Anxiety is an experience that our bodies create to help us feel prepared to deal with threat. When we feel anxious, our muscles can feel tight, we can lack appetite, and we sometimes feel a little ill. We may have trouble sitting still, feel dizzy, and our hearts may race from time to time. We might also have a dry mouth, feel uneasy, have difficulty sleeping, and have cold sweaty hands and feet. It is uncomfortable feeling anxious, and if we feel anxious for too long we can become exhausted by it.

Assessing your anxiety

We would like to recommend before you start using CBT that you make a record of your symptoms of anxiety. Type in the website address shown below into your internet browser. This will take you to an assessment page.

z1b6.com/7.html

When you complete this assessment, you will find that it gives you scores in seven areas. You can keep track of your progress in each of these areas as you complete CBT exercises by noting down your scores at regular intervals. You can then see how the CBT exercises that you use alter the way that you feel.

It can also be helpful to keep a more detailed record of your anxiety for a short period (maybe over a period of a week), so that you can become more aware of how your anxiety changes on a daily basis. Most of the time our memory is not very good when it comes to remembering what things affect our mood. Often the most accurate way to assess our mood is to make a record while we are experiencing it. There may also be several areas of your life that have a significant impact on your anxiety (that you are unaware of). Keeping track of your anxiety will help you to identify what areas of your life are keeping your anxiety in place. If you notice regular changes in your mood, this is a potential area for you to talk over with your psychiatrist/family doctor. We have placed a sheet on the next page that you can use to measure your mood changes quite accurately.

Anxiety Diary

Please use this diary to keep a record of your feelings of being relaxed and anxious. For each time period give yourself a score between 0 and 10 where 10 is the most that you can experience a feeling.

For the relaxed feeling box please rate how relaxed you felt during each time period as a whole.

For the anxious feeling box please rate how anxious you felt during the time period.

Day	Date	
Time period	Anxious feeling 0 to 10	Relaxed feeling 0 to 10
6am-12pm		
12pm-6pm		
6pm-12am		

Day	Date	
Time period	Anxious feeling 0 to 10	Relaxed feeling 0 to 10
6am-12pm		
12pm-6pm		
6pm-12am		

Day	Date	
Time period	Anxious feeling 0 to 10	Relaxed feeling 0 to 10
6am-12pm		
12pm-6pm		
6pm-12am		

Day	Date	
Time period	Anxious feeling 0 to 10	Relaxed feeling 0 to 10
6am-12pm		
12pm-6pm		
6pm-12am		

Day	Date	
Time period	Anxious feeling 0 to 10	Relaxed feeling 0 to 10
6am-12pm		
12pm-6pm		
6pm-12am		

Day	Date	
Time period	Anxious feeling 0 to 10	Relaxed feeling 0 to 10
6am-12pm		
12pm-6pm		
6pm-12am		

Day	Date	
Time period	Anxious feeling 0 to 10	Relaxed feeling 0 to 10
6am-12pm		
12pm-6pm		
6pm-12am		

Day	Date	
Time period	Anxious feeling 0 to 10	Relaxed feeling 0 to 10
6am-12pm		
12pm-6pm		
6pm-12am		

Day	Date	
Time period	Anxious feeling 0 to 10	Relaxed feeling 0 to 10
6am-12pm		
12pm-6pm		
6pm-12am		

Anxiety Diary

Please use this diary to keep a record of your feelings of being relaxed and anxious. For each time period give yourself a score between 0 and 10 where 10 is the most that you can experience a feeling.

For the relaxed feeling box please rate how relaxed you felt during each time period as a whole.

For the anxious feeling box please rate how anxious you felt during the time period.

Day _____ **Date** _____

Time period	Anxious feeling 0 to 10	Relaxed feeling 0 to 10
6am-12pm		
12pm-6pm		
6pm-12am		

Day _____ **Date** _____

Time period	Anxious feeling 0 to 10	Relaxed feeling 0 to 10
6am-12pm		
12pm-6pm		
6pm-12am		

Day _____ **Date** _____

Time period	Anxious feeling 0 to 10	Relaxed feeling 0 to 10
6am-12pm		
12pm-6pm		
6pm-12am		

Day _____ **Date** _____

Time period	Anxious feeling 0 to 10	Relaxed feeling 0 to 10
6am-12pm		
12pm-6pm		
6pm-12am		

Day _____ **Date** _____

Time period	Anxious feeling 0 to 10	Relaxed feeling 0 to 10
6am-12pm		
12pm-6pm		
6pm-12am		

Day _____ **Date** _____

Time period	Anxious feeling 0 to 10	Relaxed feeling 0 to 10
6am-12pm		
12pm-6pm		
6pm-12am		

Day _____ **Date** _____

Time period	Anxious feeling 0 to 10	Relaxed feeling 0 to 10
6am-12pm		
12pm-6pm		
6pm-12am		

Day _____ **Date** _____

Time period	Anxious feeling 0 to 10	Relaxed feeling 0 to 10
6am-12pm		
12pm-6pm		
6pm-12am		

Day _____ **Date** _____

Time period	Anxious feeling 0 to 10	Relaxed feeling 0 to 10
6am-12pm		
12pm-6pm		
6pm-12am		

What is CBT?

CBT is a scientifically supported treatment. Scientists have used CBT techniques with thousands of people, measured the results very carefully, and found out that it works to help most people with psychological distress to feel better (at least for a couple of years). The ideas behind CBT were developed by several people, but the most famous people involved with it in the early stages were Aaron Beck, a psychiatrist, and Albert Ellis a psychologist.

When people do CBT they complete exercises to change the way a) they think, b) they behave, and c) that they react to their feelings. For many people this results in an improvement in mood. People can do CBT on their own, online, or they can do it with a therapist, although evidence suggests that CBT tends to work much better with a therapist. Reading CBT books like this one can also help a little. CBT helps people to make connections between their thoughts, their physiological reactions (or how their body reacts), their emotions, and their behaviour. Once people become aware of these connections, they can then make little changes here and there to feel much better about themselves.

Brain organisation

To use CBT effectively you will need to know how three important parts of the brain communicate with each other. In this book we will refer to these brain areas as the thinking mind, the feeling mind, and the thoughts and emotions regulator, (see Figure 1).

The thinking mind

The thinking mind, also known as the neocortex, is a part of the brain responsible for thinking, planning, and logical thought. We use this part of the brain to understand and use language, to make calculations, and to problem-solve. This part of the brain is used a lot in complex thought.

The feeling mind or the primitive/animal mind

The feeling or primitive mind (also known as the subcortical region of the brain) is located in the middle/bottom of the brain. It is often referred to as the primitive or animal brain, as we share similar brain structures with other mammals. The primitive brain's main focus is survival. The limbic system (a part of the primitive mind) and the areas beneath it are where emotions initially begin. The amygdala (see Figure 2) in particular, which is located on both sides of the brain, activates emotions such as anxiety.

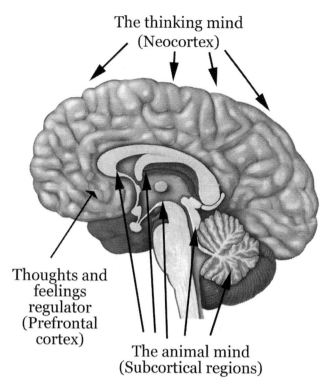

The thinking mind
(Neocortex)

Thoughts and
feelings
regulator
(Prefrontal
cortex)

The animal mind
(Subcortical regions)

Figure 1. Basic brain organisation

The thoughts and feelings regulator

The thoughts and feelings regulator – technical name prefrontal cortex – is an essential part of the brain that helps to maintain good mental health. The thoughts and feelings regulator's job – or the regulator for short – is to sit next to lower areas of the brain, acting as a communication system between the thinking mind and the primitive mind. It has many important functions. It quietens down noise in the mind and it can call off emotional reactions started in lower regions of the brain. We also use this part of our brain to think about our thinking and to make choices.

The regulator often stops working properly for short periods when people become highly anxious; this can lead to individuals with anxiety feeling that their mind is foggy or that they cannot think clearly. In depression, the regulator can stop working for much longer periods of time, contributing to poor concentration and difficulties with attention.

What happens when we experience threat?

The primitive mind becomes highly active when we experience perceived threat, (whether real or imagined). When this occurs it releases neurochemicals or brain chemicals known as catecholamines, which improve the way that it functions. In simple terms, catecholamines work like a turbo boost or a 'power-up' for the primitive brain. When primitive brain regions become more active, we become

6

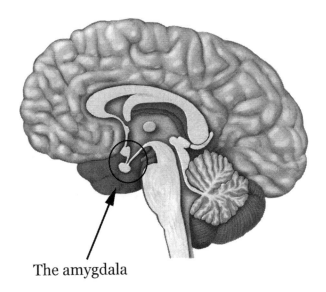

The amygdala

Figure 2. Location of the amygdala

more aware of all of our senses. As a result of this, we may see, hear, feel, taste, and smell things more strongly (Guzman, Tronson, Jovasevic Sato, Guedea, Mizukami, Nishimori, & Radulovic, 2013).

This 'power up' process is not without problems, however. Catecholamines, although improving the effects of the primitive region of the brain, spread into the nearby regulator and stop it functioning effectively. This spreading effect is usually only temporary; when the threat dies down and the brain chemicals are reabsorbed the regulator starts to work normally as before.

What happens when we experience threat for long periods of time?

If we experience threat for long periods of time the continuous release of catecholamines by the primitive mind can gradually damage (or cause decay to) the regulator located right next to it (Arnsten, Raskind, Taylor, & Connor, 2015). (This generally results in the regulator working much less effectively.) When the regulator goes offline or begins to work less effectively, we lose our ability to calm ourselves and we can begin to feel more anxious about things that we weren't really bothered about before. The thinking mind is also unable to function effectively as it relies heavily on the regulator to help it make decisions and to direct attentional resources. This is generally why therapists tell their clients not to make any important decisions about their lives until they have recovered from their mental health problems.

In summary, when people experience short-term anxiety reactions they can't think straight and their minds go foggy. The thinking mind is not able to function properly, as to do this it needs the assistance of the regulator to hold ideas in mind, and to think about thoughts at the same time. When the regulator comes back online again, people tend to find that they are able to think clearly once more. This occurs in all of us regardless of how intelligent we are.

'I can't believe how difficult the homework for 11-year-olds is these days.'

We worry more when we are anxious

Worrying (or asking ourselves 'What if? questions) is a type of problem-solving process that many of us use to highlight feared situations or outcomes. Ironically, many of us worry because we want to feel safe. We think that if we know the worst things that could happen to us, then we won't be caught off guard and we can put things in place to be prepared.

Worry, however, elevates our estimation of risk. When we feel more at risk we are more likely to look out for threat-based information and worry even more. When this occurs, streams of frightening thoughts activate the primitive mind's threat responses, which in turn begins to shut down the regulator. (This is important to note, because as we have already mentioned, one of the regulator's jobs is to quieten noise in the mind.) With the regulator offline we begin to access more irrational thoughts and we can find ourselves stuck in a worry loop (see Figure 3).

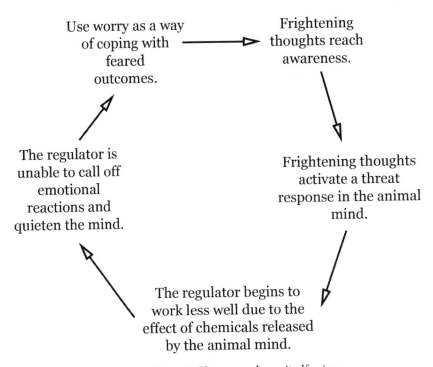

Figure 3. How worry keeps itself going

How different parts of the brain communicate with each other

Our feeling or primitive mind listens in to all of our higher-level thoughts in order to keep our bodies a little ahead of us, preparing us physically for whatever we might need to do next. If we think about eating a lemon, our mouths will start to salivate slightly. This happens before we get anywhere near a lemon.

'Hey wait! I said it's getting dark...Not park!'

In many respects, one way to think about how different parts of the brain talk to each other is to think of the brain as like a horse and a rider. The primitive mind is the horse. The horse provides the power to take the rider wherever he or she wants to go. The horse understands basic language, but is always on the 'lookout' for danger and will speed up if it notices any kind of threat. The thinking mind is the rider. The rider decides a) the direction, b) where to go, and c) what is a threat and what isn't. The regulator is the equipment that the rider uses to manage the horse. The equipment is the saddle, reigns, stirrups, whip, blinkers, and such like.

In short, completing CBT for anxiety is very much like learning how to ride a nervous horse. Once the rider has developed a relationship with the horse, the rider can learn how to a) calm the horse if the horse gets startled, and b) stop the horse taking over and/or bolting. Ostensibly, we will be using CBT to teach the thinking mind how to communicate effectively with the primitive mind.

The brain works holistically

The brain is holistic, which means that most parts of it work at the same time, or in parallel. Most brain areas are also directly connected to other brain areas, with information travelling between different points in microseconds. As a result, the primitive brain, where anxiety springs from, has immediate access to a) every thought that occurs within the thinking mind, and b) all sensory information.

Not all information generates anxiety in the animal mind just thoughts and sensory information that are viewed as a threat at a primitive level. Thoughts and sensory information that produce anxiety in the primitive mind are therefore likely to be connected to our safety, our social conduct, our financial future, reproduction, health, physical security, friendships, family, food, and social status.

Avoidance and safety behaviours

The use of avoidance and safety behaviours are very common habits for people who experience anxiety. Avoidance involves deliberately staying away from situations that might create emotional distress. Safety behaviours are strategies that people use to reduce their distress when they approach situations that they fear. Both avoidance and safety behaviours tend to keep people's problems in place; as time progresses continued use of them can lead to a gradual loss of self-esteem and self-confidence.

Many people are skilled in finding ways to control or stop their anxiety and become experts in developing strategies to avoid it or get rid of it. This behaviour is not surprising, not only due to our natural inclination to avoid high levels of distress, but also because it's normal to want to avoid potentially harmful outcomes.

How overuse of avoidance and safety behaviours causes problems

There is a major problem with using avoidance and safety behaviours where anxiety is concerned. This is because the more we use safety behaviours, the more automatic safety behaviours and avoidance strategies become. It is natural for us to experience a sense of relief when we carry out a behaviour that removes pain or reduces worry. In psychological terms, this process is referred to as negative reinforcement. Negative reinforcement occurs when we carry out certain behaviours to remove painful feelings. Over time, as processes are repeated and memory pathways are laid down, we begin to carry out these same behaviours automatically without thinking (see Figure 4 & Figure 5).

Figure 4. Negative reinforcement

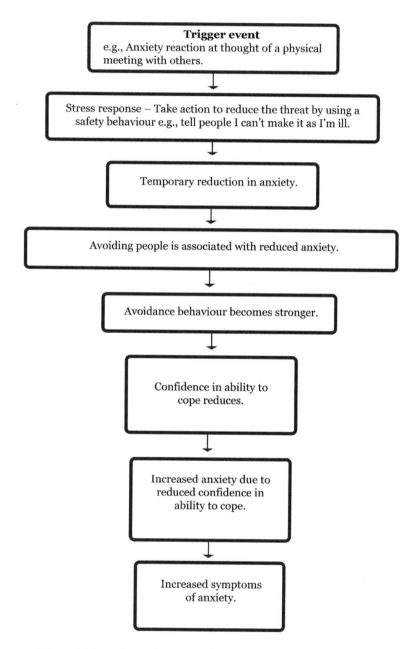

Figure 5. More advanced example of negative reinforcement in action

What kinds of safety behaviours are people naturally likely to use when they are distressed?

We have drawn up lists of the most common safety behaviours and avoidance patterns that people with different forms of anxiety experience. If you have already completed your online assessment, you could just skip to the problem areas that concern you the most.

Social anxiety

Estimates vary, but it is suggested that between 5% and 15% of Western individuals will suffer with social anxiety during part of their lifetime. The effects of social anxiety are not the same for all sufferers. For some, their social anxiety may be restricted to just one or two areas for example, public speaking, whereas for others their social anxiety can surface in multiple areas of their lives.

The major feature of social anxiety, which separates it from other forms of anxiety, is that sufferers attempt to hide their anxiety symptoms from others due to their fear of being judged negatively. To cope with a fear of being judged, many sufferers carry out numerous safety behaviours; for example, monitoring themselves, attempting to hide their anxiety, etc.

Examples of safety behaviours associated with social anxiety

- Use diazepam, a drug that alters neurotransmitter functioning to produce a calming effect, or beta-blockers before social events e.g., business meetings.
- Carry a supply of diazepam just in case.
- Drink alcohol before going out to relax.
- Avoid situations where social anxiety has occurred in the past or where it may occur in the future.
- Go to the toilet before going out (related to fear of using lavatories and others overhearing lavatory use).
- Have someone with you when going to social situations.
- Carry a bottle of water to help with a dry mouth.
- Sit close to an exit, so as to escape unnoticed.
- Hold onto or lean onto something supportive to hide shaking or trembling.
- Wear light clothing, fan self, or stand near a window or a doorway to prevent overheating. Alternatively, wear more clothes to conceal sweating.
- Have tissue ready to wipe hands to conceal sweaty hands.

- Use heavy make-up to avoid others noticing blushing or cover face with hair.
- Drink out of a bottle rather than a glass to avoid others noticing shaking hands.
- Have stories ready to put on an act of social competence and to have something interesting to say.
- Focus on the self to assess social performance.
- Avoid conversations with people.
- Stand in a corner to keep a low profile.
- Keep conversations as short as possible to avoid revealing anything that could be self-incriminating.
- Focus on appearance.
- Try to control facial expressions.
- Avoid eye contact with others.
- Mentally rehearse what is being said before it is said.
- Have excuses about a need to leave pre-planned and ready.

Panic attacks

A panic attack is a whole-body response to perceived threat or danger. The bodily sensations experienced in panic attacks are particularly strong, and they mainly occur when there is no obvious physical danger. In a state of panic, physical changes occur very quickly, including an increase in heart rate, contraction of the digestive system, sweating, bodily trembling, and breathing changes.

Examples of safety behaviours associated with panic attacks

- Use diazepam, or beta-blockers before certain situations, e.g., using public transport, business meetings etc.
- Carry a supply of diazepam just in case.
- Do not move too fast due to fear of heart rate increase.
- Drink alcohol before going out to relax.
- Avoid situations where a panic attack has occurred in the past or where one may occur in the future.
- Do not eat before going out if related to a fear of vomiting.
- Go to the toilet before going out if related to fear of losing control of bowels.

- Have someone with you when in potential situations where panic could occur.

- Carry a brown paper bag to breathe in and out of.

- Carry a bottle of water in case of dry mouth.

- Carry a plastic bag if related to fear of vomiting.

- Sit in places near to an exit in public places.

- Hold onto or lean onto something supportive.

- Hold breath, keep an eye on emotions.

- Fan self to stop self overheating.

- Distract self, for example by watching television.

Health anxiety

Many people worry about their health from time to time, but for individuals with health anxiety, there is often excessive worry about potential health conditions and/ or pre-existing health conditions.

People who experience health anxiety often suffer with intrusive thoughts about illness, and carry out safety behaviours to help themselves feel better. Safety behaviours may include monitoring the body for signs of illness; seeking reassurance from doctors; going onto the internet and researching symptoms; worrying about coping with serious illness; and requesting medical tests or investigations. Sometimes, however, the very behaviours that are used to reduce anxiety and to feel safe actually create more anxiety and the sufferer becomes even more preoccupied with a search for signs and symptoms of illness.

Examples of safety behaviours associated with health anxiety

- Monitor any unusual symptoms in body.

- Seek reassurance.

- Make an appointment with doctor or alternatively avoid doctors completely.

- Go onto the internet to conduct research.

- Complete online assessments to self-diagnose.

- Scan body.

- Complete exercises to check if body is working OK.

- Worry about ability to cope with various physical disorders.

- Request medical tests from doctor or alternatively avoid medical tests totally.

- Request medical checks to rule out disorders.
- Control diet.

Obsessive compulsive disorder (OCD)

Experts still do not really know what causes OCD, although most experts agree that it runs in families. At the moment, researchers think that it probably comes about through a combination of learnt behaviour, genetic vulnerability, and brain developmental problems in the womb and/or in childhood.

The main thing that separates OCD sufferers from people without it is that OCD sufferers find it very difficult to separate themselves from frightening and intrusive thoughts, images, and feelings. Intrusive thoughts often appear to come out of nowhere, carrying high levels of emotional distress with them.

There is a compulsion among OCD sufferers to reduce the intensity of their emotional experience by carrying out specific behaviours or thinking patterns. Psychologists call these compulsive responses 'neutralisers'.

Examples of safety behaviours associated with OCD

- Avoid situations or people that may trigger obsessional thoughts.
- Re-trace steps.
- Go back and check on things that you are unsure of.
- Complete ritualistic behaviour, such as touching wood to stop things from happening.
- Complete mental calculations; for example, the times tables to distract self from emotions.
- Push away intrusive thoughts.
- Complete activities a certain number of times.
- Perform activities in a particular order.
- Wear particular jewellery or make-up.
- Carry certain items.
- Check and re-check to make sure that you have not left anything behind.
- Look for reassurance from others.
- Stay with safe people.
- Clean things to avoid contamination.
- Hold onto items or hoard items.

Phobic anxiety

Individuals with phobic anxiety have involuntary fear reactions to specific environmental triggers; for example, insects, birds, trains, planes, the dark, and such like. Most commonly, sufferers develop phobic anxiety as a result of a) watching the fear experiences of others (most commonly in childhood) or b) having frightening or shocking experiences; for example, someone could develop a phobic reaction to wasps after being stung by a wasp, or someone could develop a phobia of flying after having a panic attack on a plane.

Examples of safety behaviours associated with phobic anxiety

- Avoid certain objects or places. This may be related to something frightening that happened in the past.
- Avoid certain forms of transport.
- Take specific alternative safer routes when travelling.
- Avoid certain smells, sensations, tastes, and physical feelings that produce anxiety.
- Ask for reassurance or ask others to check things for you.
- Go to places with safe people.
- Avoid watching television programmes about certain subjects.
- Try to be in control of others when you feel in an unsafe situation. For example, giving advice to others on how to drive, what to be careful of and such like.

CHAPTER 2

Observing yourself

The first stage in using CBT involves observing yourself. When you begin this process you might become aware of two things. Firstly, you might notice that you have more thoughts and feelings than you realised. Secondly, you might recognise that you have a range of thoughts, feelings, and behaviours in different circumstances. Once you become aware of this, you can monitor how you react in different situations.

Just as a professional running coach may recommend leg-strengthening exercises to athletes to enable them to run faster, we recommend that you focus on self-observation to exercise your regulator or prefrontal cortex. This will benefit you because a stronger regulator is associated with a) improved mood regulation and b) a quieter mind.

Observing yourself accurately

An important part of any scientific approach is accurate observation. From a CBT point of view, standing back and thinking about your own thinking processes will enable you to increase your awareness of your thoughts, feelings, and behaviours, particularly when you are feeling anxious. A process of self-observation can also assist you to become aware of the cycles that you fall into when you become emotional. We want to encourage you to begin to take an exploratory approach to your problems and to think about your thinking processes. We suggest that you do this because when you are able to 'think about your thinking' or when you become curious about how you think, you will feel less trapped by the content of your mind, and your mind's automatic processes. You will then have an opportunity to explore, to be curious, and to notice your thoughts without judging yourself.

Thought diaries

There are many different variations of self-observation diaries used in CBT, but most involve recording combinations of thoughts, body changes or physiological reactions, feelings/emotions, and behaviours. Diaries encourage the use of regular body scanning, which will be beneficial to you as body scanning a) improves sensory awareness and b) encourages increased experiential learning. Experiential learning occurs when you learn about yourself through your senses and feelings rather than through talking or reading. (In Chapter 12 you will find out that experiential learning is also the most effective way to teach the primitive part of the mind new ways of behaving.)

Measuring physiological reactions and emotions

In this book when we ask you to notice your 'physiological reactions', we are asking you to recognise specific changes that occur in your body. Body changes that you may notice when you are upset could be increased tension, your jaw tightening, your chest feeling tight, your head pounding, your heart racing, feeling heavy in your legs and such like. When we ask you to label your emotions we are asking you to describe the meaning you give to specific bodily changes. Many physiological reactions connected to emotions are very similar; for example, the physiological changes associated with anxiety and anger both involve a) heart rate increase, b) a rise in blood pressure, and c) tension in major muscle groups.

Thought, feeling, and behaviour sheets

If you would like to look at an example of a thought, feeling, and behaviour sheet that people fill in when they have CBT, we have placed an example on the next page from a client called David (see Table 1). David said that he was carrying around a lot of ill feeling because he had not been invited to a colleague's wedding. It appeared that his colleague had invited about half of the staff in her office to her wedding and had left many out. David had become preoccupied with being left out. Although he knew that there were good reasons why he had not been invited – his colleague had fallen out with his wife some years back – he felt that he no longer knew how to react to her when she was around him. The situation was causing him some distress.

Table 1. Example of Situation, thought, emotion, and behaviour sheet

Time: Date: Trigger situation	Thoughts, e.g., 'They must think that I'm an idiot'	Emotion, e.g., anxiety, anger, shame, disgust	Behaviour, e.g., avoid situation
2pm 9th June Felt that a friend was trying to make me feel small.	'She asked that question deliberately to try to undermine me.'	Angry, irritated. Feel agitated all over.	Made an excuse to leave the situation for 5 minutes and then decided not to return at all. Others wondered where I was and perhaps thought I was acting strangely.
1.30pm 11th June Not being invited to a colleague's wedding.	'She invited practically everyone else in the office apart from me. When she's got no one else to talk to, she wants to be my friend.'	Feel low and angry. I feel irritated being around her.	Ignore her whenever possible. Others start to think I am behaving oddly and ask me 'What's wrong?' I just say everything is fine.

A point worth noting is that you may not be able to complete thought records when you feel highly anxious. If you feel that you can't complete a thought record when you feel anxious, simply take a thought record sheet out later (when you feel less anxious) and remind yourself about what happened. Try to take your mind back to the event you are focusing on and notice what thoughts may have been going through your mind. While you do this, quickly scan your body and notice what impact your thoughts are having on the way that you feel. Following this, make a note of how you reacted (your behaviour) to your thoughts and feelings.

Why it is important to complete thought, feeling/physiology, and behaviour diaries

There are two reasons why self-observation diaries are a useful part of CBT. Firstly, they provide helpful material that people can work on (see Chapter 7). Secondly, they increase people's motivation to change by drawing attention to unhelpful thinking patterns that people get caught up in.

Generally, most of us live our lives automatically, without giving much thought to a) thinking about our thinking, b) how we react to our feelings, or c) what makes us behave the way that we do. Completing a diary brings more of these automatic processes into awareness. Once these patterns are brought into our conscious awareness, we immediately have more choice about how to react. This is due to the fact that writing down information about the self encourages processes of a) stepping back and observing, b) focused detachment, and c) self-reflection.

Another example of a thought, feeling/physiology and behaviour diary

In our second example, Michael, a football coach, found himself churning a dispute that he had with a fellow football coach over and over in his mind. In many respects, he recognised that he was not moving on from what had happened. Although he recognised that dwelling on it any further was pointless he found himself regularly returning to the dispute and playing it over and over in his mind. Michael's sheet is shown below (see Table 2).

Table 2. A situation, thought, emotion, and behaviour sheet

Day: Thursday 6th June

Time: 12.00 pm

Trigger situation: Dissagreement with another coach

Thoughts:

'He's going along with the referee's decision because it's easier for him. My reaction shows that there is something wrong with me. He's laughing at me and thinks I'm an idiot.'

Physiological reactions

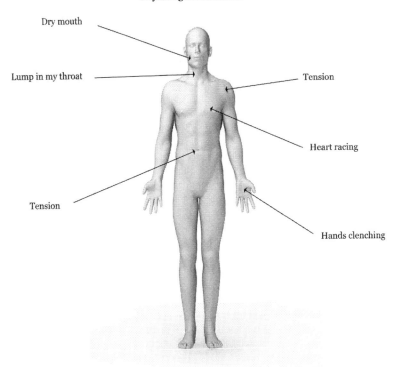

Dry mouth

Lump in my throat

Tension

Heart racing

Tension

Hands clenching

Emotion:

Anxiety, anger, guilt, shame.

Behaviour:

Raise a formal protest. Think of some different ways in which I can get him back. Churn the situation over in my mind for a couple of days. Feel guilty and ashamed about the way that I am thinking.

Behaviour, e.g., avoid situation		Emotion, e.g., anxiety, anger, shame, disgust		Thoughts, e.g., 'They must think that I'm an idiot'		Time: Date: Trigger situation	

Thought, emotion, physiology, and behaviour sheet

Day: **Time:** **Trigger situation:**	**Thoughts:**

Physiological reactions

Emotion:	**Behaviour:**

CHAPTER 3

Cognitive distortions

When we become anxious, the brain changes the way it operates. Emotions heavily influence the way that we think, the way that we view the world, and the way that we behave. Much of the time when we feel anxious our minds are affected by processes known as cognitive distortions. Cognitive distortions are changes in our mental perception that, can at times give us a skewed view of the world. Cognitive distortions can move our thinking style from being balanced, flexible, expansive, and considering to a more rigid style, not dissimilar to that which you might expect from small children.

Cognitive distortions can lead us to think that we can see the future.

'Looks like it's going to be terrible tonight. I think I'd better stay in.'

Or we can make things much bigger or smaller than they really are.

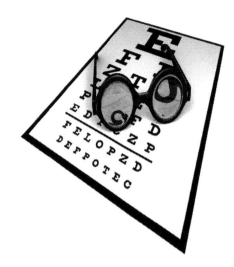

Our cognitive distortions can also make our world appear as if it is a very dangerous place to live in.

We advise, that when you complete thought records, you assess whether cognitive distortions are occurring so that as time progresses you can learn how to detach from them. We have placed a table of some of the more common thinking distortions on the next page (see Table 3).

We have also placed a blank situation, thoughts, and cognitive distortions records sheet at the end of this chapter for you to copy and work through. Place as much focus as possible on recording situations where you feel anxious. Write down your thoughts at the time, and look to see how many thought distortions you can find.

Thinking biases and what to look out for

All or nothing thinking: Viewing things as either right or wrong; there is no middle ground. Things are either perfect or fundamentally flawed. There is just black or white, grey does not exist, e.g., always/never, good/bad.

Personalising: Focusing on things in the immediate environment and connecting it to the self. Thinking for example, 'She did that deliberately because she knew that I wouldn't like that!' The world revolves around the self.

Mental filtering: Selecting specific negative ideas to dwell on and ignoring all of the positive ones.

Disqualifying the positive: Positives don't count, there is nothing special about the way I did it, e.g., 'That only happened because I was lucky.'

Distorted images: Using images as evidence. A picture or image in the mind that reflects extreme themes of fear, sadness, disgust, pain, etc.

Fortune telling: Predicting the future in a negative way without any real evidence, e.g., 'It's going to be terrible'; 'It will be a disaster'; 'I just know it.'

Shoulds, oughts, & musts: Having ideas that things can only be done one way: 'People should ...'; 'I must ...'; 'I really ought to ...'; 'He shouldn't have ...'

Over-generalising: Taking single events or circumstances and viewing them as happening more often than they really do. Thinking that things happen everywhere.

Emotional reasoning: Using emotions as evidence, e.g., 'I feel it, so it must be true.'

Mind reading: Drawing conclusions about what others are thinking without any evidence, e.g.; 'She doesn't like me'; 'They think I am stupid.'

Situation, e.g., an interpersonal issue	Thought, e.g., 'She asked that question deliberately to try to undermine me!'	Thought distortion, e.g., mind reading

CHAPTER 4

Rules

CBT often focuses on the rules that people hold. We all live by rules and most of the time our rules help us. They work automatically in the background of our minds, guiding us through social situations and occasions. We have literally hundreds of rules that guide our behaviour or our expectations; for example, we have rules about queuing up, how we and others should drive our cars, what is expected when we are in a restaurant, what clothing is worn at particular locations, etc. Most of the time we are completely unaware of our rules unless someone breaks them; for example, if somebody pushes in front of us in a queue, talks loudly in a library and such like.

> 'When I first started having CBT I noticed that my rules were mainly about how I wanted others to perceive me. I was a bit surprised when I found out how rigid my rules were. I kind of knew they were there in the background but I hadn't really given them much thought before therapy. They were something along the lines of "If I produce results and I am contributing at all times, then I will be OK". And, "If I meet the highest standards at all times then I will be OK"' My rules meant that I spent most of my time working and not spending time with my family. If I wasn't working I felt as though something wasn't quite right. I found it difficult to stop and rest even for five minutes. If I stopped working I felt guilty or anxious. It felt wrong if I wasn't achieving something.'

When you complete CBT it is often useful to notice the rules that you have, especially the kinds of rules that can leave you feeling distressed, upset, anxious, guilty, or angry. We have placed rule record sheets in this chapter for you to record what rules you hold for yourself and what rules you hold for others. We have also included a rule challenging sheet for you to complete if you choose to (for a completed example see Table 3). Sometimes rules are difficult to recognise. Close friends and family members will help you to notice what your rules are if you ask them: sometimes it is easier to see other people's rules than our own.

'I tended to get irritated, anxious, and angry if my rules were broken, often making life difficult for others as well as myself. My rules were something like:

"If nobody is upset with me and everybody likes me at all times, then I will be OK."

"If I work hard and achieve at all times, then I will be OK."

"If I am in control at all times, then I will be OK."

"If I am strong at all times, then I will be OK."

"If people are happy with my performance, then I will be OK."

"If I am the best at what I do, then I will be OK."

"If people don't let me down, then I will be OK."

During the time that I struggled the most I took on very difficult tasks and generally worked until I became exhausted. When I wasn't able to work the way I did before, I felt guilty about not working and started beating myself up over it. In therapy, when I thought about what was happening it really brought to my attention what I was doing. I thought I was doing all the extra work to help others and my family, but obviously it didn't feel that way to them. Ironically, in my attempts to prove to myself that I was OK, I ended up upsetting most of the people that I came into contact with.'

'Your colleagues tell me that you are a concrete thinker, so I made your job description using these.'

Rule sheet: Use the box to the right to note which rules apply to you	✔
If I am in control at all times, then I will be OK	
If people are happy with me at all times, then I will be OK	
If I do things perfectly at all times, then I will be OK	
If I am the best at what I do at all times, then I will be OK	
If I don't experience any unusual bodily sensations, then I will be OK	
If I am feeling good at all times, then I will be OK	
If I am feeling confident at all times, then I will be OK	
If I am not blamed for things, then I will be OK	
If I show dominance at all times, then I will be OK	
If I perform well at all times, then I will be OK	
If I am physically well at all times, then I will be OK	
If I am assertive at all times, then I will be OK	
If I know what I am doing at all times, then I will be OK	
If I know what is going to happen at all times, then I will be OK	
If I appear to others as though I know what I am doing, then I will be OK	
If I feel safe at all times, then I will be OK	
If I appear competent at all times, then I will be OK	
If I show no signs of vulnerability, then I will be OK	
If I am in control of my feelings at all times, then I will be OK	
If I say 'Yes' to all requests at all times, then I will be OK	
If I am strong at all times, then I will be OK	
If things go wrong it is all my fault	
If I don't let people down, then I will be OK	
If I can fix things, then I will be OK	
If I am in control of my body at all times, then I will be OK	
Total number of rules endorsed (write total number of rules endorsed in right-hand column)	

Rule sheet: Use the box to the right to note which rules apply to you	✔
If others don't challenge me, then I will be OK	
If people are happy with me at all times, then I will be OK	
If people around me don't make any mistakes, then I will be OK	
If others tell me that I am the best at what I do at all times, then I will be OK	
If people around me are happy, calm, and relaxed, then I will be OK	
If people around me are polite and respectful, then I will be OK	
If people around me are confident, then I will be OK	
If others don't criticise me, then I will be OK	
If others let me take charge, then I will be OK	
If people around me appreciate me, then I will be OK	
If people around me tell me that I am alright, then I will be OK	
If people listen to me at all times, then I will be OK	
If people around me know what they are doing at all times, then I will be OK	
If others reassure me, then I will be OK	
If others show confidence in me at all times, then I will be OK	
If others help me feel safe, then I will be OK	
If others approve of me at all times, then I will be OK	
If others show no signs of vulnerability, then I will be OK	
If others put my needs ahead of their own, then I will be OK	
If others say 'Yes' to my requests when I ask them, then I will be OK	
If I am around strong people, then I will be OK	
If others take the blame for mistakes, then I will be OK	
If others don't let me down, then I will be OK	
If others can fix things for me, then I will be OK	
If others are there for me when I need them, then I will be OK	
Total number of rules endorsed (write number of rules endorsed in right-hand column)	

Table 3. An example of a rule challenging exercise

Rule If others are happy with me, then I will be OK.

How real and familiar does the rule feel?

It feels real a lot of the time. It feels as though it is part of me.

What impact does the rule have on your life?

A lot of my goals are focused on things I need to do to keep other people happy.

It makes me easy to manipulate and once people realise I am like that they will often use it to make me feel bad so that I will do what they want.

What benefits does this rule have on your life?

Generally, most people seem to be unhappy with me at some point so I guess it just makes me feel miserable.

Were you born with that rule?

No.

How old is the rule?

I guess about 40 years old.

Where do you think the rule came from?

I learnt it from my parents.

If you learnt the rule from a person, where do you think he or she learnt it from?

I think my parents learnt it from their parents. It seems to be stronger on my father's side of the family.

Do you want to keep that rule?

Definitely not.

If you gave yourself an opportunity to have another rule, what rule would you pick?

Other people are responsible for their own happiness. I am responsible for my happiness. I can help others, or give advice to others, but they are responsible for their own feelings.

How do you think you will feel if you choose to believe your new rule as much as the old one?

I would feel as though I am not continually failing to please others. I would feel more relaxed.

How does knowing that you can choose to have another rule make you feel?

It feels a little alien. It feels a little hard-hearted. But I feel better because I know logically this will create less stress and I will feel better and it will actually be more beneficial to others in the long term.

Rule challenging exercise

Rule

How old is the rule?

If you gave yourself an opportunity to have another rule, what rule would you pick?

How real and familiar does the rule feel?

Where do you think the rule came from?

What impact does the rule have on your life?

How do you think you will feel if you choose to believe your new rule as much as the old one?

If you learnt the rule from a person, where do you think he or she learnt it from?

What benefits does this rule have on your life?

How does knowing that you can choose to have another rule make you feel?

Do you want to keep that rule?

Were you born with that rule?

CHAPTER 5

Beliefs

Generally speaking, limiting beliefs are deeply held ideas about the self that we fear might be true. By the time that we become adults, our beliefs can become so deep-set that we may feel that they define who we are. We may also hold rules and carry out numerous 'safety behaviours' to protect ourselves from them without being aware of it. Most of us do not realise that, in fact, our beliefs run us and guide a lot of our thinking patterns as well as our behaviours.

> 'Early on in my CBT therapy I discovered that one of my limiting beliefs was "I am a failure". The funny thing about it was no matter how hard I worked or how much I achieved, the belief "I am a failure" was always still there. It seemed like what I had done in the past counted for nothing. Trying to prove the belief wrong demanded so much of my time that it affected my health. I didn't realise it was driving me so much. I didn't feel in control of my life. It drove me to do more and more. I didn't really know how to stop.
>
> My therapist helped me to notice that in many situations I was experiencing high levels of anxiety that were inconsistent with the situation that I was faced with. For example, we identified that I had an over-the-top reaction to even small amounts of criticism. After this she helped me recognise that the belief "I am a failure" was the main driver for my emotional reaction. This emotional reaction was the primitive part of my brain trying to protect me from being a failure. After I became aware of this, if I noticed my emotions were too extreme or I felt I wanted to over-react in any situation, I usually had to force myself to take a minute out to see if a limiting belief was influencing me.'

Identifying limiting beliefs*

To identify limiting beliefs, start by remembering a time when your emotional response or behavioural reaction was much greater than you feel the situation demanded. You can follow this by completing a CBT exercise known as a *downward arrow*. With a downward arrow exercise you keep following your feelings and thoughts until you reach the deepest fear that you hold about yourself. We have placed an example of a downward arrow exercise on the next page, (see Figure 6).

There is also a blank downward arrow diagram at the end of this chapter that you can photocopy. *We recommend that you do not complete this exercise by yourself unless you have already completed CBT with a therapist.

The definition of 'to believe' is accepting that something is true without evidence or proof.

Downward arrow exercise

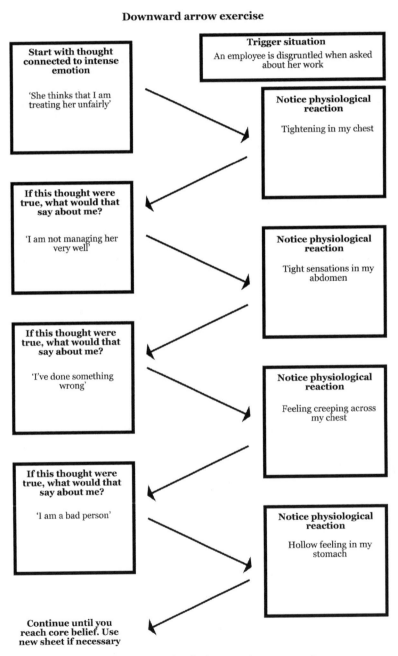

Figure 6. An example of a downward arrow exercise.

Downward arrow exercise

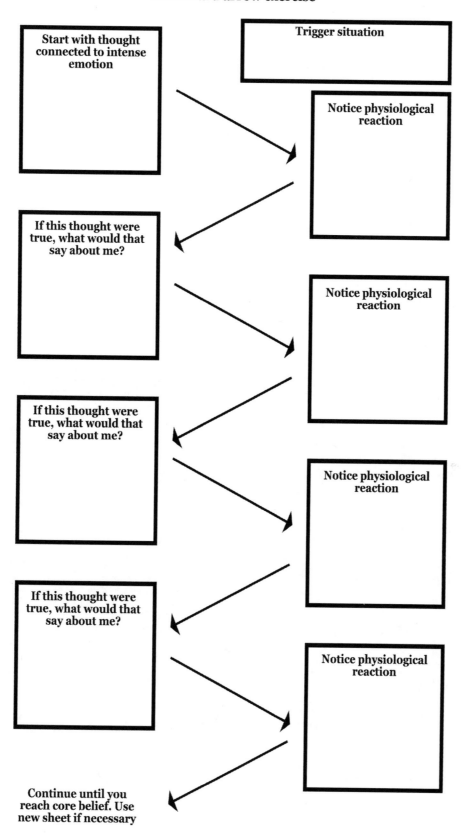

Start with thought connected to intense emotion

Trigger situation

Notice physiological reaction

If this thought were true, what would that say about me?

Notice physiological reaction

If this thought were true, what would that say about me?

Notice physiological reaction

If this thought were true, what would that say about me?

Notice physiological reaction

Continue until you reach core belief. Use new sheet if necessary

CHAPTER 6

Drawing out beliefs, rules, and behaviour cycles

A useful starting point will be to make a connection between your beliefs, rules, and safety behaviours (see Figure 7 below).

'One of my rules was "If I am successful at all times and if people are happy with my work at all times then I will be OK". The main things I did were to work very long hours, make sure I did everything perfectly, not take breaks, compare my work with others to make sure that I was the best, and get angry if anybody made suggestions about improvements (see Figure 7).

Beliefs
'I am a failure'

Rules
'If I am successful at all times and people are happy with me, then I will be OK.'

Behaviours

Work very long hours.
Make sure I do everything perfectly.
Don't take breaks.
Compare my work with others to make sure that I am the best.
Get angry if anybody makes sugestions about improvements.

Figure 7. An example of a connection between beliefs, rules, and behaviours

'My therapist asked me what happened when I felt I could not keep to my rule of being successful at what I did at all times. I told her this made me feel highly anxious and on edge. We worked out that I was getting these feelings because my belief "I am a failure" was being activated when I was not maintaining my rule. When this happened, I felt that I needed to do what I was doing before even more to protect myself from my fear of failure. This led to me working even harder. Eventually, I worked so hard that I became exhausted and depressed.

My therapist asked me about how my very best attempts at proving to myself that I wasn't a failure, may have actually ended up with me believing that I was a failure even more. It's a bit obvious when I describe it now, because I'm not in it, but my partner was unhappy with me. My life felt like a mess and I felt that I was failing in all areas of my life (see Figure 8).'

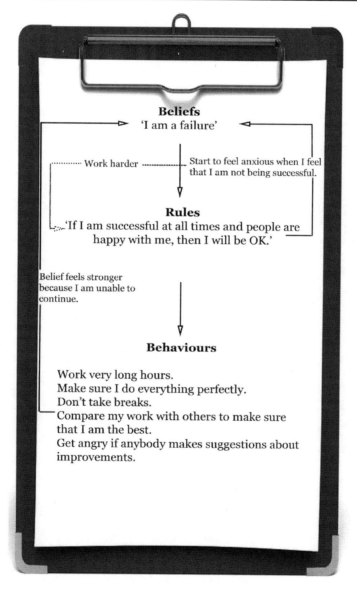

Figure 8. A more developed example

38

Drawing out your own beliefs, rules, and behaviour cycle

To draw your own cycle, the best place to start is by noticing what triggers your anxiety. Your anxiety trigger does not need to be a major event. It could be anything that makes you feel anxious, such as noticing an unusual symptom in your body (as occurred for Jane, see Figure 9), or obtaining some poor results at work (as occurred for Nicola, see Figure 10). In CBT language we refer to these triggers as critical incidents.

Once you have identified your critical incident, scan your rule sheet and notice which of your rules may have been broken. In our completed example (see Figure 9), Jane's rules were connected to her believing that she needed to be in control of her body at all times. For Jane, when her body reacted in ways that she did not understand or when she felt she was not in control of her body this activated her beliefs that she was 'not safe', 'weak', and 'defective'.

After you have identified which of your rules may have been broken, next look at your behaviour: this is what you do to keep your rules in place. For example, with Jane, this involved her monitoring her body for any unusual sensations. For Nicola, this led to her criticising herself and working even harder.

Finally, think to yourself about how your behaviours may reinforce what you fear most about yourself. In Jane's case, her safety behaviours led to her feeling less confident and avoidant, whereas for Nicola, despite all her hard work, she never noticed or acknowledged her achievements.

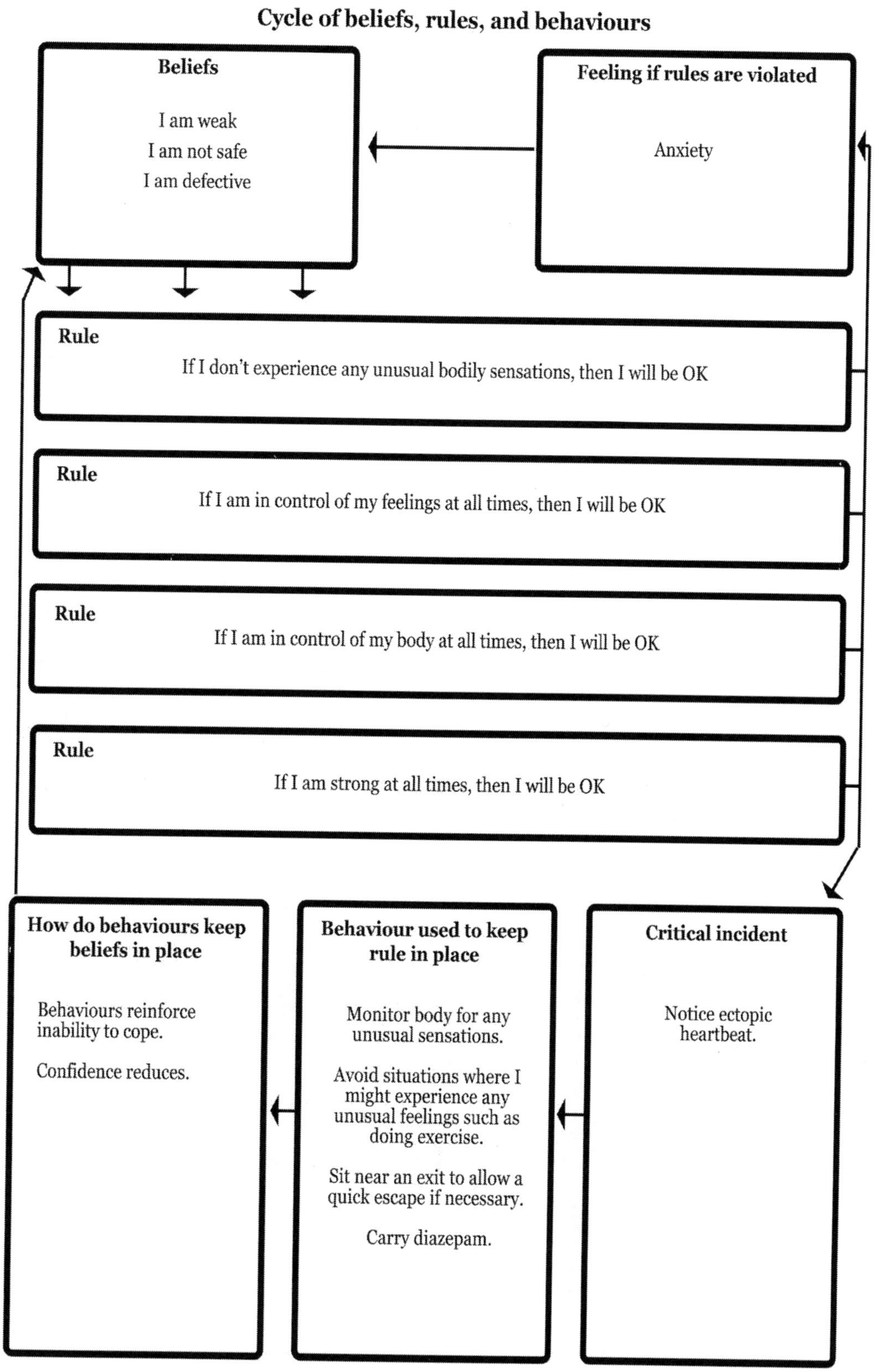

Cycle of beliefs, rules, and behaviours

Beliefs

I am weak
I am not safe
I am defective

Feeling if rules are violated

Anxiety

Rule

If I don't experience any unusual bodily sensations, then I will be OK

Rule

If I am in control of my feelings at all times, then I will be OK

Rule

If I am in control of my body at all times, then I will be OK

Rule

If I am strong at all times, then I will be OK

How do behaviours keep beliefs in place

Behaviours reinforce inability to cope.

Confidence reduces.

Behaviour used to keep rule in place

Monitor body for any unusual sensations.

Avoid situations where I might experience any unusual feelings such as doing exercise.

Sit near an exit to allow a quick escape if necessary.

Carry diazepam.

Critical incident

Notice ectopic heartbeat.

Figure 9. Jane's cycle of beliefs, rules, and behaviours

Cycle of beliefs, rules, and behaviours

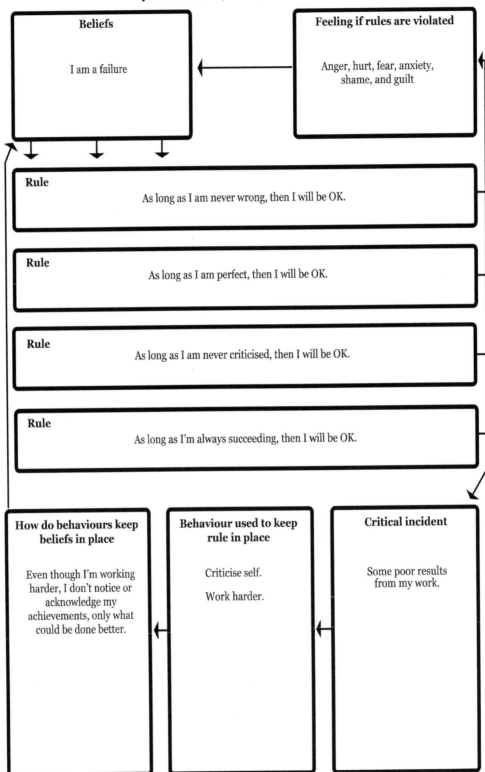

Beliefs	Feeling if rules are violated
I am a failure	Anger, hurt, fear, anxiety, shame, and guilt

Rule
As long as I am never wrong, then I will be OK.

Rule
As long as I am perfect, then I will be OK.

Rule
As long as I am never criticised, then I will be OK.

Rule
As long as I'm always succeeding, then I will be OK.

How do behaviours keep beliefs in place

Even though I'm working harder, I don't notice or acknowledge my achievements, only what could be done better.

Behaviour used to keep rule in place

Criticise self.

Work harder.

Critical incident

Some poor results from my work.

Figure 10. Nicola's cycle of beliefs, rules, and behaviours

Cycle of beliefs, rules, and behaviours

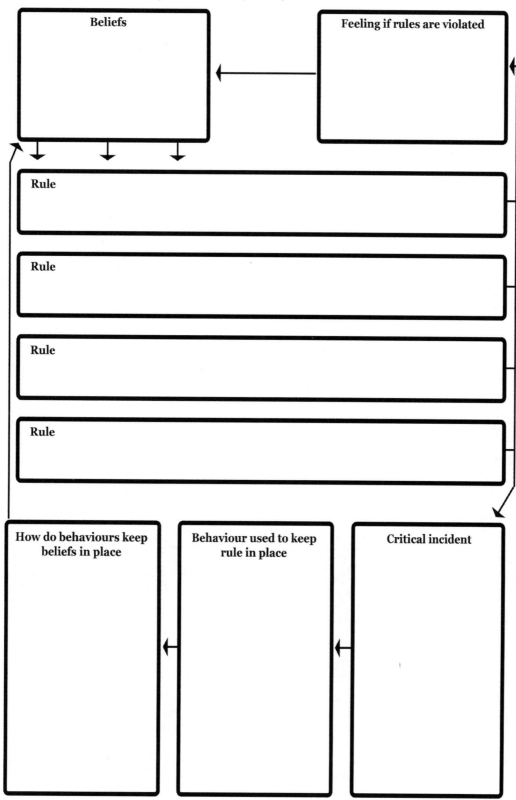

CHAPTER 7

CBT cycles for anxiety

There are several ways of drawing out CBT cycles in CBT. Cycles can be drawn differently according to the problems that you are experiencing. We have included many of the most common cycles in this chapter.

The traditional CBT cycle

A traditional thoughts, feelings, and behaviour cycle is a starting point for many people in understanding how CBT models work. Writing down your thoughts, feelings, and behaviours and placing them in cycles, will increase your ability to be self-observant. The process of self-observation alone can have a big impact on your thinking processes and speed up your recovery from mental health problems. The traditional cycle is designed to help you recognise that thoughts can have a significant impact on emotions, emotions can influence behaviour, and behaviour can determine thoughts and feelings. Although drawing out this cycle will not resolve your difficulties, it will increase your awareness of your problems, and this will increase your motivation to make changes. We have placed David's information into a traditional cycle (see Figure 11).

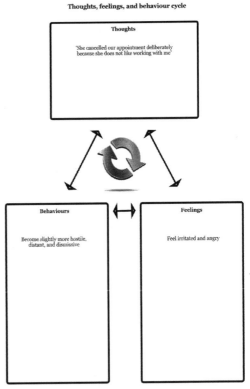

Thoughts, feelings, and behaviour cycle

Thoughts

'She cancelled our appointment deliberately because she does not like working with me'

Behaviours

Become slightly more hostile, distant, and dismissive

Feelings

Feel irritated and angry

Figure 11. An example of a traditional CBT cycle

Thoughts, feelings, and behaviour cycle

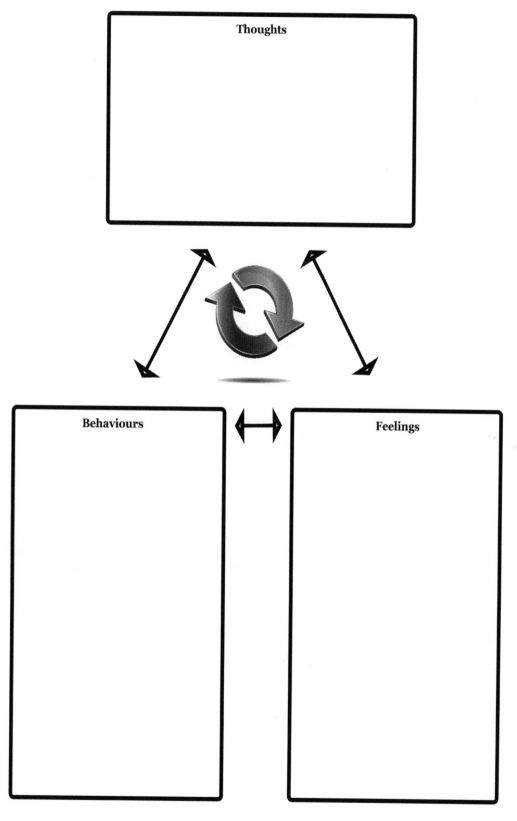

Thoughts

Behaviours

Feelings

The generic CBT cycle

The most commonly used CBT cycle is called the generic thoughts, feelings, behaviour, and physiology cycle. In this cycle, thoughts influence feelings and physiology, feelings and physiological changes influence behaviour, and behaviour reinforces thoughts.

An example of a generic CBT cycle

Vera, 68, had been anxious for a couple of months before she attended an assessment appointment with her therapist. Her therapist noticed very quickly that Vera worried a lot about what others thought of her; in particular, that others might view her as weak and incapable. Vera worked for a couple of hours a week as a volunteer in her local village shop, and this work had given her a lot of satisfaction. She said that her job had given her a lot of enjoyment in the past because it had been an opportunity for her to catch up with the local villagers and to find out what had been going on in her neighbours' lives. On one particular day she was thinking about phoning up her shop manager and cancelling her stint in the shop. She thought this might be a good idea because she hadn't quite been herself due to her symptoms of anxiety and she was concerned about what others might think of her. We have placed her thoughts, feelings, physiology, and behaviour in a generic cycle on page 46 (see Figure 12).

The trigger point for Vera was looking at her calendar and noticing that she had a shift in the shop coming up.

How to complete a generic CBT cycle

Before you fill in a generic CBT cycle it is usually practical to have a completed thought diary ready, so that you have a range of thoughts to work with (see Chapter 2). A good place to start is to look through the thoughts in your diary and pick out a thought that produces the most distressing emotion.

Once you have selected a thought, keep the thought in your mind for a little while and then complete a body scan. A body scan will involve you bringing your awareness to your body and noticing physiological changes and emotions that accompany the thought. The meaning behind the thought can be identified by asking yourself 'If this thought were true, what would it say or mean about me?'

A CBT cycle can be especially useful in bringing to mind how self-fulfilling prophecies work. This will then naturally lead on to the completion of thought challenging exercises, which will be covered in Chapter 9.

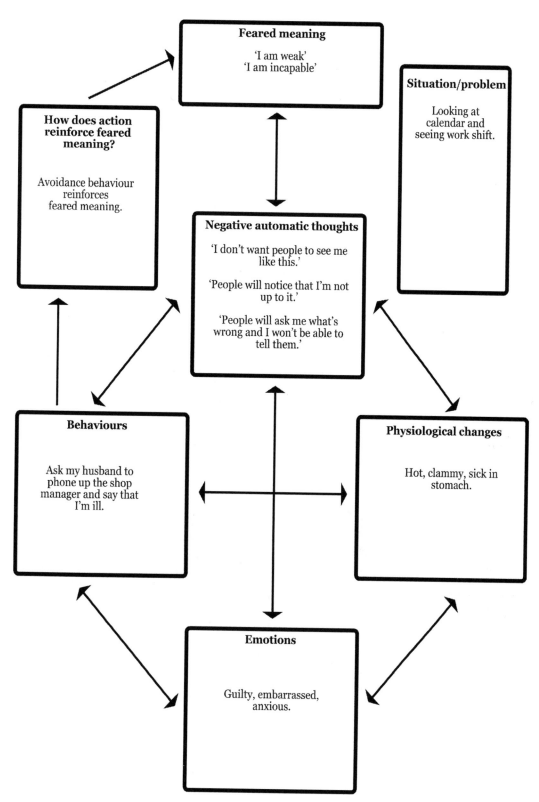

Figure 12. Vera's generic CBT cycle

Another example of a generic CBT cycle

Gerry, a builder, had requested CBT to help him deal with his procrastination, which was affecting several different areas of his life. Gerry was looking to find a way to help him deal with his procrastination over invoicing clients. Gerry said that he hated this part of his work, and he tended to put it off until he had very little money in the bank. Putting off invoicing tended to cause quite a few problems for him, as the longer he left his invoicing the more difficult it was for him to collect money that was due to him. This increased his anxiety further still (see Figure 13).

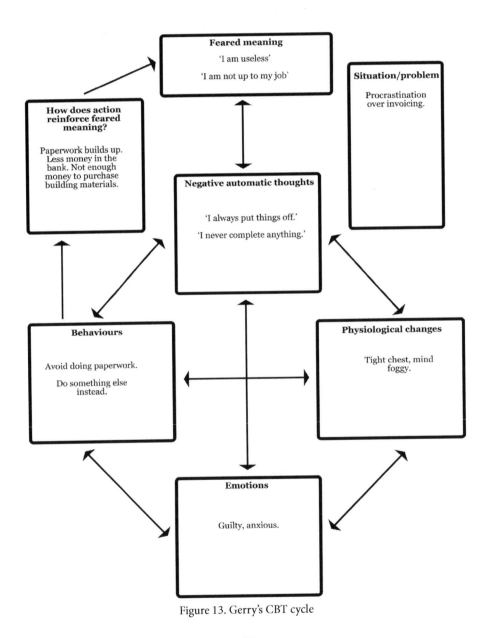

Figure 13. Gerry's CBT cycle

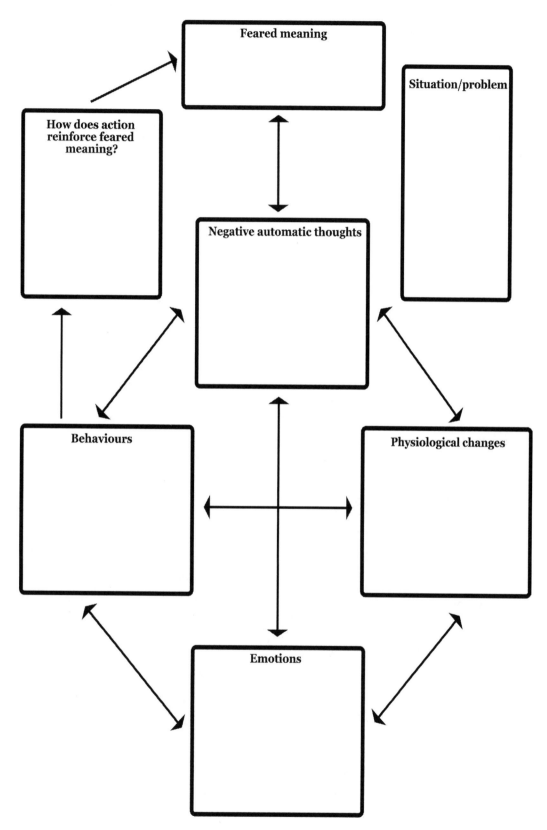

Social anxiety cycles

CBT models of social anxiety suggests that a social anxiety experience starts with a trigger situation that activates an individual's beliefs and assumptions: usually this is a belief that the individual is defective, weird, odd, or abnormal (Clark & Wells, 1995). This creates a feeling of anxiety, leading the individual to carry out safety behaviours, with the most commonly used behaviours being self-focus and self-monitoring. Cognitive models draw attention to the safety behaviours that sufferers use and point out that the use of such safety behaviours leads to increased symptoms of social anxiety and an even greater belief that the sufferer is weird, strange, or odd.

An example of a CBT model for social anxiety

To demonstrate a CBT model for social anxiety, we will look at the case of Jemma, 15. Jemma had been experiencing social anxiety for a while before she was referred for a course of CBT. She told her therapist that her main concerns were a) her relationship with her boyfriend and b) whether she could manage the stress the relationship was causing her. Jemma said she found sitting with her boyfriend's family and having family meals with them excruciatingly painful. She told her therapist that in these situations she felt highly self-conscious and embarrassed. In particular, she was concerned about blushing in front of others. She mentioned that she often monitored her face to work out whether or not it was feeling hot. She wanted to be approved of, but deep down was concerned that others would think that she was odd or abnormal. She said that if she felt her face becoming hot she would often try to fan her face to keep it cool or leave the table to go to splash water on her face. Jemma tried to avoid family meals wherever possible, as sitting down at the table felt like torture for her. Her lack of ability to handle her situation was making her feel that there was something seriously wrong with her.

We have placed Jemma's information into a beliefs, rules, and behaviour cycle (see Figure 14). Following this we have also placed Jemma's information into a generic cognitive model (see Figure 15). As you will see when you look at the latter example, we have made one simple change to the generic CBT model. We have added one area dedicated to self-monitoring and self-focus, which is common to all sufferers of social anxiety.

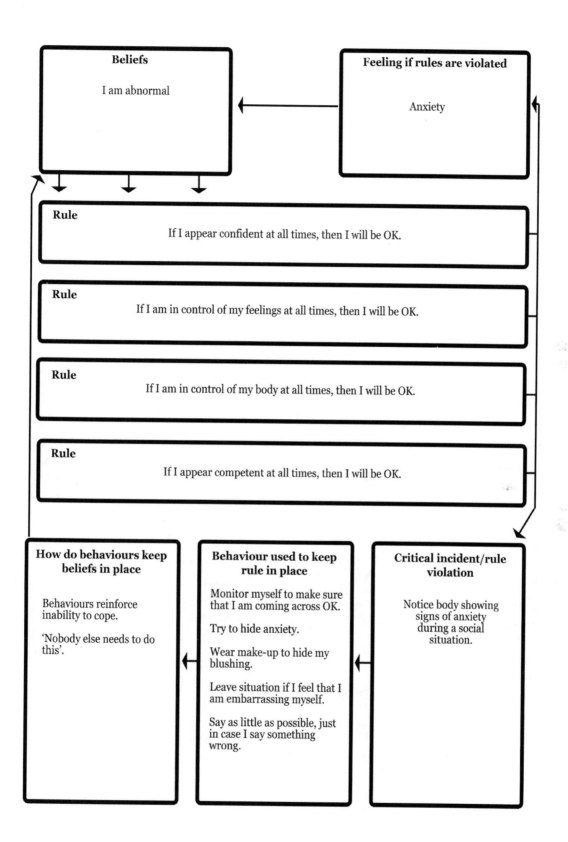

Figure 14. An example of social anxiety

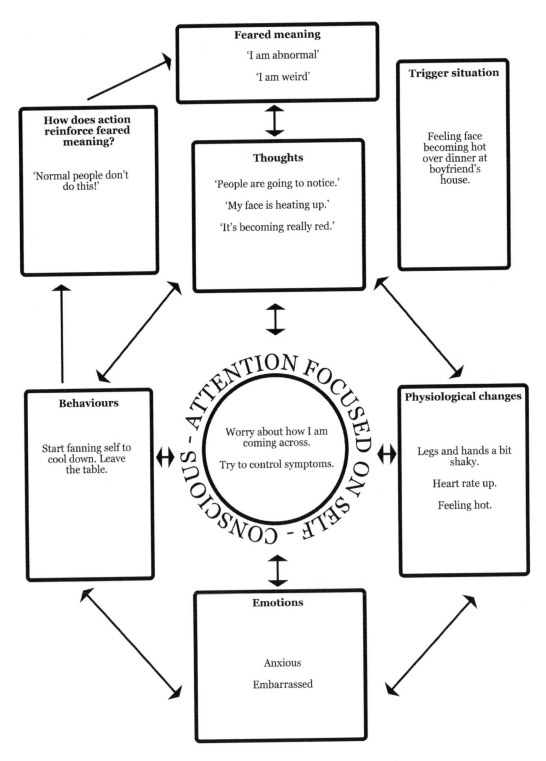

Figure 15. An example of social anxiety (adapted)

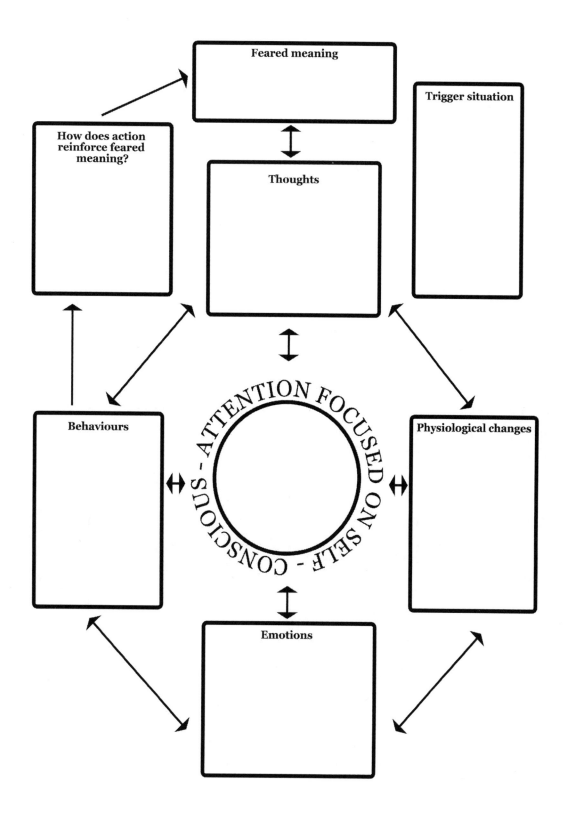

Health anxiety cycles

The 'vicious flower model' (Moorey, 2010; Wilson & Veale, 2009) is often used as an analogy to explain how the habits used by people with health anxiety end up with the sufferer feeling worse. The general idea is that although carrying out safety behaviours may feel appealing, safety behaviours actually magnify symptoms and distress levels.

An example of health anxiety

Jenny, aged 54, came to see her therapist after being referred by her general practitioner. She told her therapist that she had always been health anxious, but that her health anxiety had increased following her adult children leaving home, and after hearing that a close friend had been diagnosed with cancer. She said that she now had more time on her hands, and this had probably led to her spending more time worrying about her health.

Jenny explained that her symptoms increased after she experienced a sharp pain in her head one day. Jenny said that she went onto the internet to research her symptoms and by the end of her search process had become thoroughly convinced that she had a brain tumour. She tried to ignore what she had found out on the internet, telling herself that she was just anxious, but the thought that she might have brain cancer had become a preoccupation. Jenny then started to check how her brain was feeling on a regular basis, which led to her feeling even more concerned that her symptoms were getting worse. Eventually, Jenny sought reassurance from her general practitioner, who organised some tests for her that came back negative.

We have placed Jenny's information into a beliefs, rules, and behaviours cycle (see Figure 16) and into our version of the vicious flower model (see Figure 17).

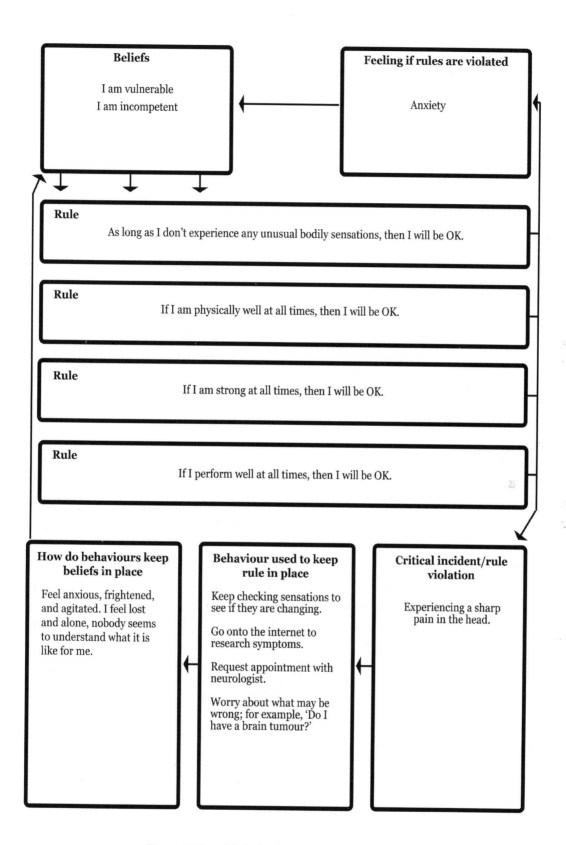

Beliefs

I am vulnerable
I am incompetent

Feeling if rules are violated

Anxiety

Rule

As long as I don't experience any unusual bodily sensations, then I will be OK.

Rule

If I am physically well at all times, then I will be OK.

Rule

If I am strong at all times, then I will be OK.

Rule

If I perform well at all times, then I will be OK.

How do behaviours keep beliefs in place

Feel anxious, frightened, and agitated. I feel lost and alone, nobody seems to understand what it is like for me.

Behaviour used to keep rule in place

Keep checking sensations to see if they are changing.

Go onto the internet to research symptoms.

Request appointment with neurologist.

Worry about what may be wrong; for example, 'Do I have a brain tumour?'

Critical incident/rule violation

Experiencing a sharp pain in the head.

Figure 16. Jenny's belief, rules, and behaviour cycle

Health anxiety maintenance model

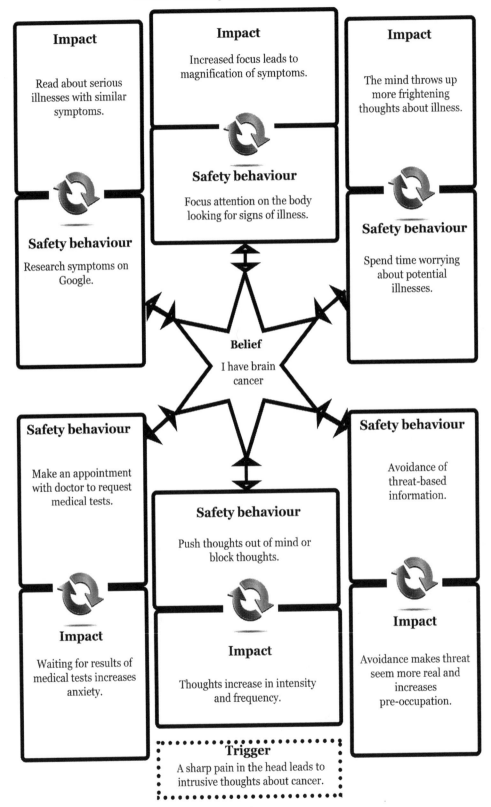

Figure 17. Jenny's health anxiety cycle

Health anxiety maintenance model

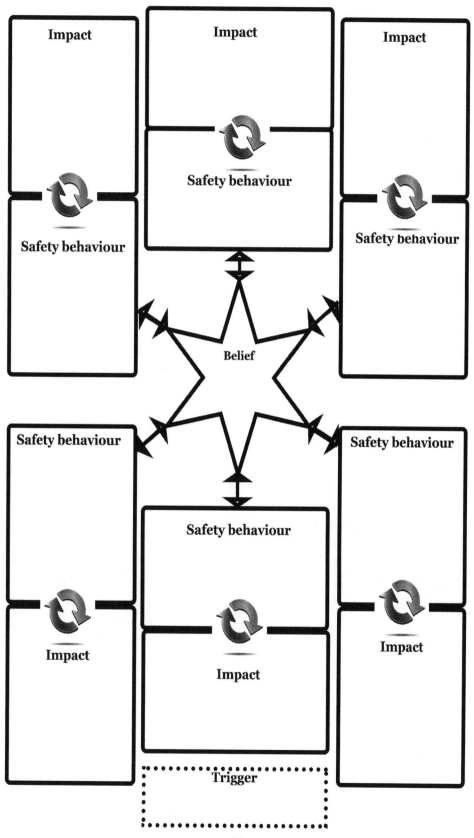

OCD cycles

OCD models of anxiety suggest that it is sufferers' reactions to intrusive thoughts that is the most significant factor in the maintenance of OCD (Rachman, Coughtrey, Shafran, & Radomsky, 2014), rather than their experience of intrusive thoughts. This has been suggested because research has found that most people without OCD have intrusive thoughts, but can easily dismiss them as 'just thoughts' (Abramowitz et al., 2014). In contrast, people with OCD find it very difficult to dismiss their thoughts, and often use their thoughts as evidence that something bad has happened or is going to happen.

OCD models begin with a trigger, which often occurs in the individual's environment: for example, walking past a used condom on the street. (Triggers are different depending on how OCD manifests itself.) Rachman et al. suggest that the real issue is how intrusive thoughts are interpreted, especially if intrusive thoughts are used as evidence that something dangerous has happened, something awful might happen, or that there is something seriously wrong because the person has had such a thought. CBT models suggest that OCD sufferers attempt to neutralise or get rid of intense emotion by carrying out a neutralising behaviour or by avoiding certain things. Over time, as these processes are repeated and memory pathways are laid down, OCD sufferers begin to carry out neutralising behaviours automatically, without thinking.

An example of OCD

Peter, 24, had experienced OCD since the age of 13. For the most part he had a normal life, but from time to time he experienced quite intense episodes of anxiety. His anxiety episodes mainly tended to occur when he was going through major life transitions, such as moving schools (when he was younger), leaving home to go to university, and forming new intimate relationships.

Peter's OCD had taken many different forms over the years, although a central theme was that somehow harm might come to his family. A lot of Peter's ritualistic behaviour was carried out to keep people safe. We have placed Peter's beliefs, rules, and behaviours cycle on page 58 (see Figure 18). We have also placed Peter's information into a traditional CBT cycle for OCD (see Figure 19), and into a more developed CBT cycle for OCD (see Figure 20).

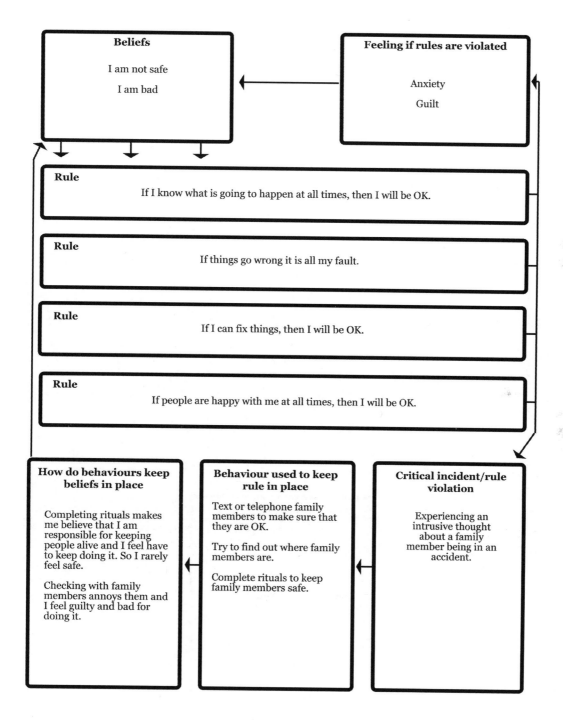

Beliefs

I am not safe

I am bad

Feeling if rules are violated

Anxiety

Guilt

Rule

If I know what is going to happen at all times, then I will be OK.

Rule

If things go wrong it is all my fault.

Rule

If I can fix things, then I will be OK.

Rule

If people are happy with me at all times, then I will be OK.

How do behaviours keep beliefs in place

Completing rituals makes me believe that I am responsible for keeping people alive and I feel have to keep doing it. So I rarely feel safe.

Checking with family members annoys them and I feel guilty and bad for doing it.

Behaviour used to keep rule in place

Text or telephone family members to make sure that they are OK.

Try to find out where family members are.

Complete rituals to keep family members safe.

Critical incident/rule violation

Experiencing an intrusive thought about a family member being in an accident.

Figure 18. Peter's beliefs, rules, and behaviour cycle

Standard OCD model

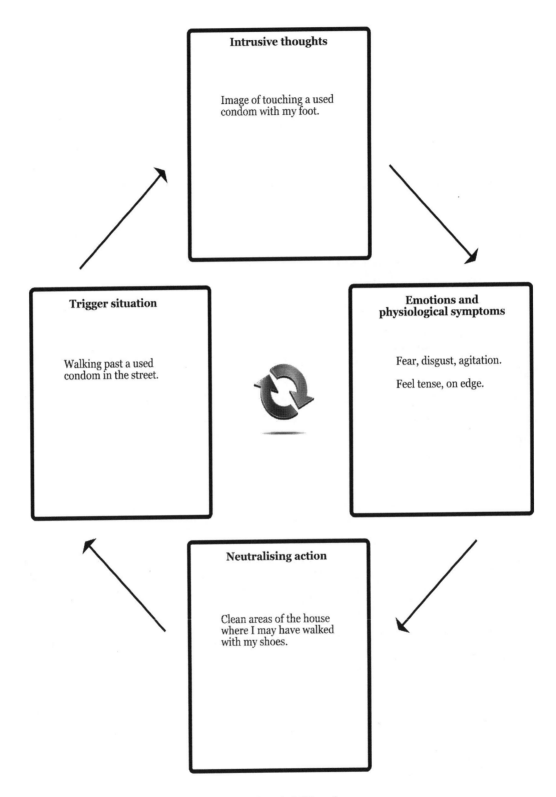

Figure 19. Peter's OCD cycle

Alternate OCD model

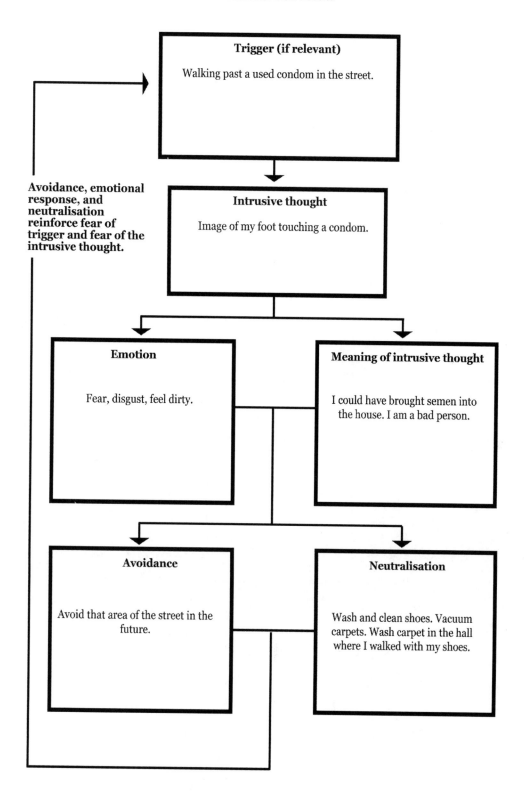

Figure 20. An alternative OCD cycle

60

Standard OCD model

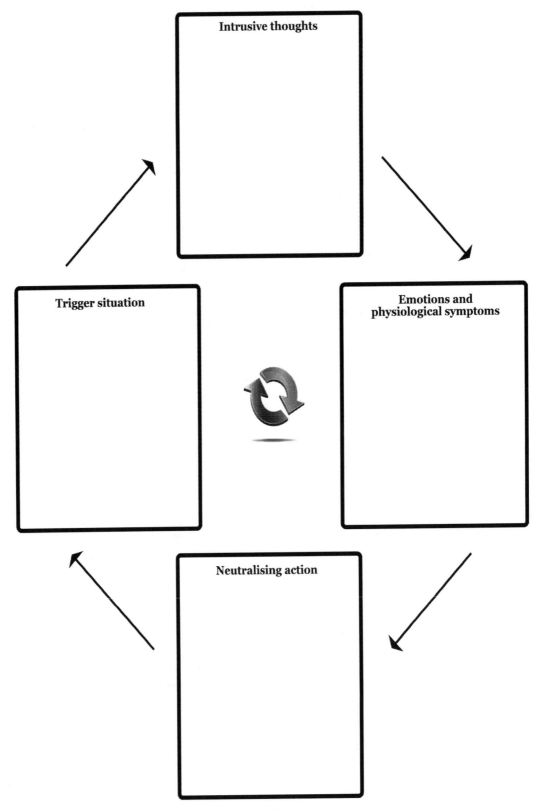

Alternate OCD model

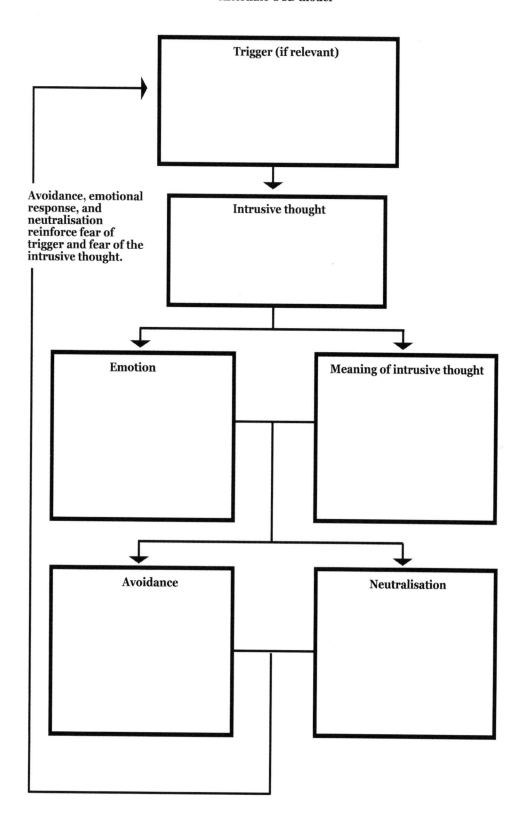

CBT cycles for panic attacks

The main feature of a CBT model for panic that distinguishes it from other CBT maintenance cycles is that it includes catastrophic misinterpretations of symptoms of anxiety (Clark 1986). Catastrophic misinterpretations occur when people use their panic symptoms (e.g., a rapidly beating heart) as evidence to support their deepest fears (e.g., 'I am having a heart attack'). The prefrontal cortex/regulator tends to shut down in panic, leaving primitive (subcortical) regions of the brain more dominant. Dominance of the primitive regions of the brain leaves people unable to access logical, analytical thought. When this occurs, people find that they have an increased tendency towards carrying out habitual behaviour – or in other words, doing what they have always done before. The final result can be that people experience panic cycles repetitively, which can be exhausting and draining, reducing the individuals ability to function.

An example of panic

Kay, a 37-year-old accountant, worked in a highly stressful job. She came for therapy after suffering panic attacks for several months. Kay told her therapist that she had experienced her first panic attack while driving home from work one evening. She said that her panic experience had come as a complete shock to her and she was still struggling to make sense of what had happened. She said that she immediately visited her family doctor, who completed several medical tests on her, before telling her that she had experienced a panic attack. Kay was confused at her doctor's diagnosis, as she had never experienced any mental health problems before. By the time of her assessment, Kay had become preoccupied that she might suffocate or pass out if she had a panic attack, and had become increasingly avoidant in several areas of her life.

We have placed Kay's information into a beliefs, rules, and behaviour cycle, (see Figure 21) and into an adapted generic CBT model (see Figure 22). The main difference between the adapted generic model (for panic) and the standard generic model is that we have added a central section for catastrophic misinterpretations. We have included this because in all experiences of panic there tends to be a catastrophic misinterpretation in some form, whether it is fear of having a stroke, dying, suffocating, passing out, etc.

Cycle of beliefs, rules, and behaviours

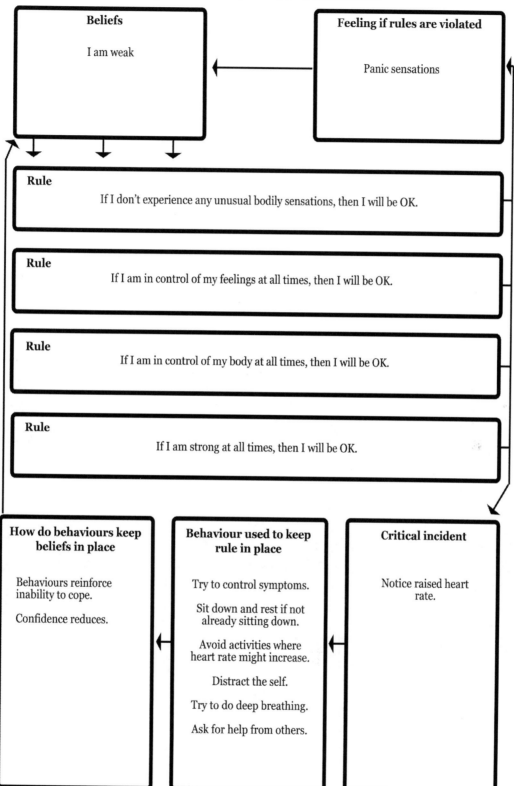

Beliefs	Feeling if rules are violated
I am weak	Panic sensations

Rule

If I don't experience any unusual bodily sensations, then I will be OK.

Rule

If I am in control of my feelings at all times, then I will be OK.

Rule

If I am in control of my body at all times, then I will be OK.

Rule

If I am strong at all times, then I will be OK.

How do behaviours keep beliefs in place

Behaviours reinforce inability to cope.

Confidence reduces.

Behaviour used to keep rule in place

Try to control symptoms.

Sit down and rest if not already sitting down.

Avoid activities where heart rate might increase.

Distract the self.

Try to do deep breathing.

Ask for help from others.

Critical incident

Notice raised heart rate.

Figure 21. Example of a beliefs, rules, and behaviours cycle for panic

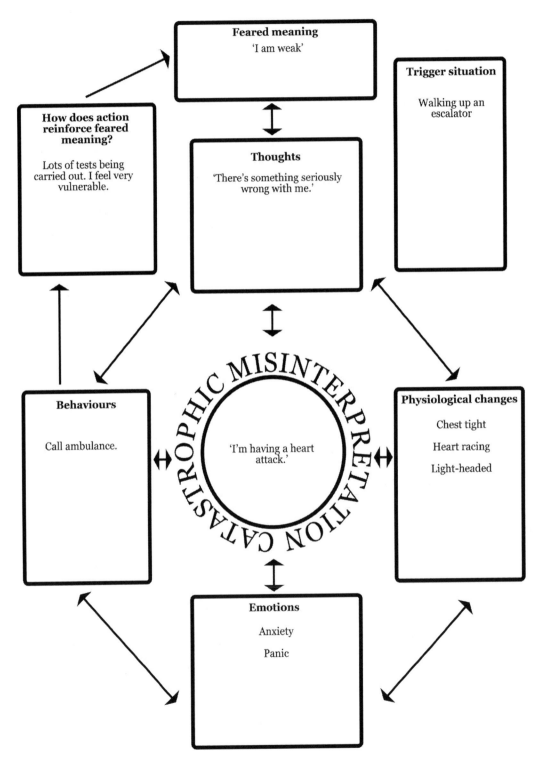

Figure 22. Example of a cycle for panic

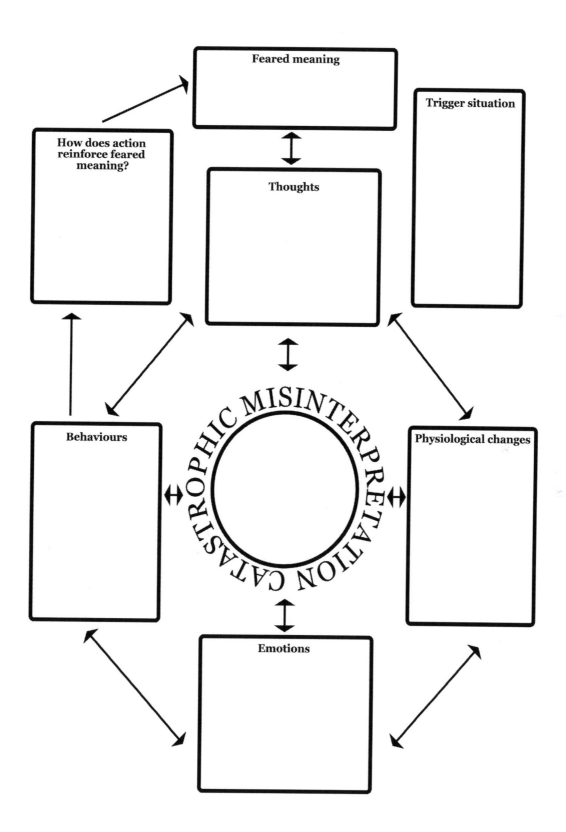

66

Manning & Ridgeway's self-phobic model

Several individuals feel panicky but do not come close to experiencing a full-scale panic attack. It is more difficult to apply panic models in such cases. Many individuals are hyper-vigilant to their bodily reactions and often take action quickly in an attempt to control their body's reactions. This can result in individuals a) excessively monitoring their body in a pre-emptive fashion; for example, recording their blood pressure and pulse, and b) becoming increasingly avoidant of activities that may result in a change in their body state; for example, not engaging in exercise as it results in a heart rate increase. The whole process leads to an increase in a) self-vigilance, and b) fear of one's own body's reactions. Problems are maintained as a result of an increase in phobic reactions to one's own body's reactions.

We have placed an example of a self-phobic reaction below using an adapted generic cognitive model (see Figure 23). In this case we have simply removed the words 'catastrophic misinterpretation' and replaced them with 'self-phobic response' and added a behaviour of 'increased vigilance over the body'.

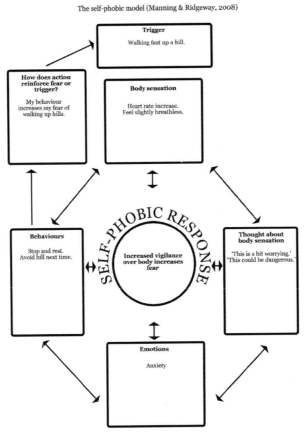

Figure 23. Example of a self-phobic response

The self-phobic model (Manning & Ridgeway, 2008)

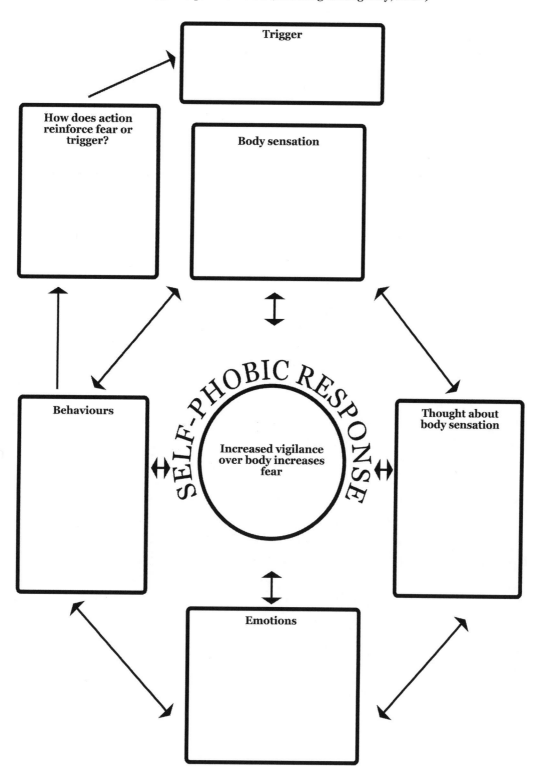

CHAPTER 8

Breaking cycles

The first step after noticing cycles is to move onto breaking cycles. A cycle can be broken by directing attention to any one area of a cycle. This is because each part of a cycle is dependent on other parts to keep it in place. For example, if avoidant behaviour is challenged this creates less opportunities to mull over negative thoughts. If feeling sad is soothed away there is less tendency to mull over negative thoughts. If negative thoughts are challenged or dampened there is less intense emotion. It is hard for a cycle to maintain itself if even one piece of it are missing.

In the chapters that follow we will show you how you can break different parts of an anxiety cycle, one step at a time, (see Figure 24). As you gather experience and skill you will gradually work towards breaking your anxiety cycles from several different angles at the same time.

To give yourself an idea of what you are working towards you could begin to think about how you would like things to be. What you would like to believe about yourself? How would you like to think? How would you like to behave? To show you how this might work we have included an example of an 'old and new' beliefs, rules, and behaviour sheet in this chapter (see Figure 25). On one side of our diagram we have placed an old cycle and on the other side we have placed a new cycle.

We have also included a blank template in this chapter for you to complete your goals for a new cycle. A tip when completing your new cycle will be to think 'What do I want?' rather than 'What don't I want?

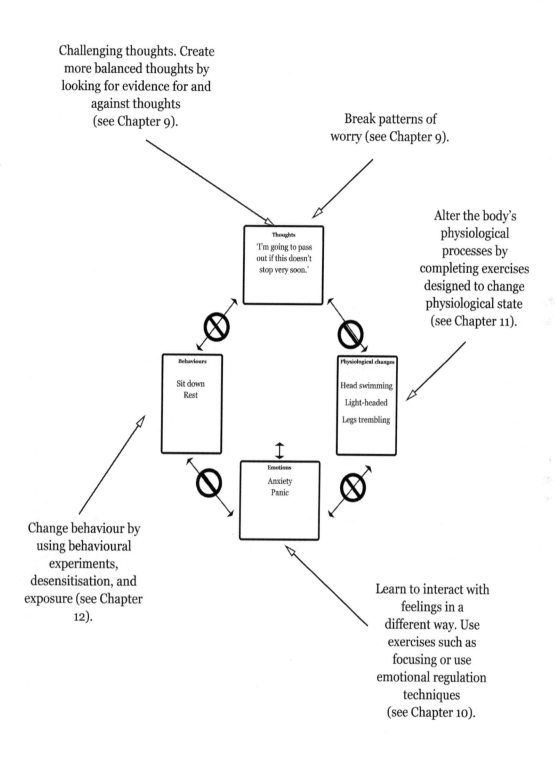

Challenging thoughts. Create more balanced thoughts by looking for evidence for and against thoughts (see Chapter 9).

Break patterns of worry (see Chapter 9).

Alter the body's physiological processes by completing exercises designed to change physiological state (see Chapter 11).

Thoughts

'I'm going to pass out if this doesn't stop very soon.'

Behaviours

Sit down
Rest

Physiological changes

Head swimming

Light-headed

Legs trembling

Emotions

Anxiety
Panic

Change behaviour by using behavioural experiments, desensitisation, and exposure (see Chapter 12).

Learn to interact with feelings in a different way. Use exercises such as focusing or use emotional regulation techniques (see Chapter 10).

Figure 24. Breaking an anxiety cycle from several different angles

Old cycle/new cycle

Past	Future
Old beliefs 'I am incompetent' 'I am not likeable' 'I am insignificant'	**New beliefs** 'I am OK' 'I am me' 'I am free'

↓

Old rules	New rules
If I am in control of my environment at all times, then I will be OK. If others like me at all times, then I will be OK. If I am in control of my feelings at all times, then I will be OK. If others notice my achievements at all times, then I will be OK.	It's normal to tell people how I feel. It's OK to assert my needs. It's important that I make room for my feelings. It's OK to make mistakes as long as I learn from them.

↓

Old behaviours	New behaviours
Keep feelings to self. Check and double check everything. Try to predict problems before they happen. Keep problems to myself. Say 'Yes' to all requests. Concentrate on getting everything correct.	Tell others how I feel. Assert myself when I want to do something. Share problems with trusted others. Check things once or just a few times. Validate and accept my feelings. Be myself.

Figure 25. An example of a completed goal sheet

Old cycle/new cycle

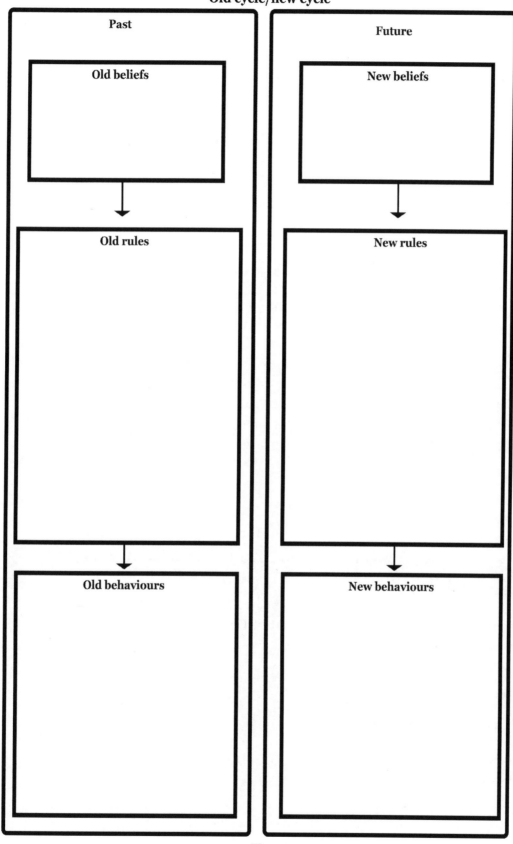

CHAPTER 9

Breaking anxiety cycles created by thoughts and images

Many of our thoughts can make us feel anxious or increase our anxiety. It is therefore important to learn ways to manage them. There are two main types of thoughts that increase anxiety: negative automatic thoughts (NATs); and intrusive thoughts. NATs are thoughts that run in the backs of our minds, creating low-level distress, whereas intrusive thoughts are highly vivid, very distressing, and barge their way into our awareness (see Figure 26). We have made some lists of common thoughts experienced by people with different anxiety conditions overleaf to give you an idea of the different types of thoughts that people experience.

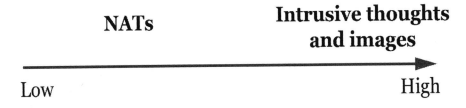

Level of emotion connected to thought

Figure 26. Intensity of emotion connected to thoughts

Some examples of thoughts and images in social anxiety

'People will find me boring.'

'My shaking will give me away.'

'People aren't interested in finding out what I have to say.'

'People won't mind if I leave early.'

'I look odd.'

'I have nothing to contribute.'

'People don't invite me anywhere.'

'I look stupid.'

'I have no social skills.'

'They won't mind if I cancel; in fact they will be relieved.'

'I am boring … Everyone is looking at me.'

'I am making a fool of myself.'

'I'm not coming across very well.'

'They can see how nervous I am.'

'I am going to say something stupid.'

'She doesn't like you, it's obvious!'

'He's trying to humiliate you.'

'My face looks like a tomato. I look ugly.'

'They think that I'm inept.'

Image of myself looking odd.

Image of others moving away.

Image of having nothing to say and looking awkward.

Image of others laughing.

Images of others feeling awkward around me.

Image of having no one to talk to.

Some examples of thoughts and images in OCD

'Something bad is going to happen.'

'Something is wrong.'

'Do it again just in case.'

'You're a paedophile.'

'You look strange.'

'If something goes wrong, it's all your fault.'

Thought of a family member being harmed.

Thought of infecting somebody with a disease.

Thought of being infected with a disease.

Thought of breathing in a dangerous substance or gas.

Thought of sexually assaulting somebody.

Thought of deliberately hurting a child.

Thought of being gay. (When the OCD sufferer is not gay.)

Image of someone having a terrible accident.

Image of myself hurting somebody.

Image of a building collapsing.

Image of a fire starting because of something I did or didn't do.

Image of a loved one being dead.

Image of myself kissing somebody inappropriately on the lips.

Image of myself being sexually inappropriate.

Some examples of thoughts and images in panic

'I'm going to die.'

'This has got to stop soon.'

'I'm going to have a stroke.'

'I'm going to lose control of myself.'

'I'm going mad.'

'I'm going to faint.'

'I'm going to suffocate.'

'I'm going to wet myself.'

'This is the end.'

Image of myself running through the street.

Image of myself panicking and everyone standing around watching not knowing what to do.

Image of wetting myself and everyone standing around looking.

Image of myself being trapped and unable to escape.

Image of myself with my heart thumping, sweating, feeling trapped, and not being able to do anything to escape.

Some examples of thoughts and images in health anxiety

'I have cancer.'

'There is something seriously wrong with me.'

'I could have an undiagnosed illness.'

'I have heart disease.'

'Do I have early signs of dementia?'

'What if the doctors have missed something?'

'It's not meant to feel like this.' (Referring to a part of the body.)

'That sensation doesn't feel right.'

'How will my family cope without me?'

'I am going to die young.'

Image of myself dying in hospital.

Image of tumour growing in part of my body.

Image of myself being dead.

Challenging NATs

When beginning thought challenging it can often be useful to start working with NATs, as the lower levels of distress that comes with them can make them easier to break down. One of the most effective ways to disrupt NATs is to bring alternative explanations to mind using a thought challenging process. To help you with this, we will describe a thought challenging process used with one of our younger clients Ben, 17.

One of Ben's NATs was 'Others will laugh at me if my hands shake'. The upshot for Ben was that he thought that if his girlfriend noticed his hands shaking she would judge him negatively and possibly end their relationship.

The first part of Ben's thought challenging process involved placing his information into a CBT cycle. In this case, we placed Ben's information into a generic CBT cycle adapted for social anxiety (see Figure 27). This offered a very clear idea to Ben about how his thoughts, feelings, and behaviour were maintaining his problem.

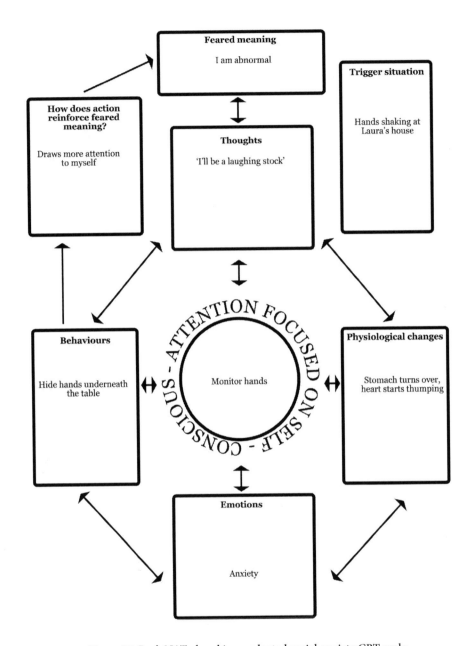

Figure 27. Ben's NAT placed in an adapted social anxiety CBT cycle

After looking at his cycle, Ben completed a thought challenging record (see Table 4). A thought challenging record is a collection of notes used to provide alternative evidence against NATs. You will find empty tables in this chapter that you can photocopy and use to challenge your NATs. NATs are placed in the first column, evidence for the NAT is placed in the second column, evidence against the NAT is placed in the third column, and a more balanced thought is placed in the fourth column.

Table 4. Ben's NAT challenging record

Negative automatic thought, for example, 'Things aren't going to work out for me'.	Evidence for negative automatic thought, for example, 'I feel that it might happen.'	Evidence against negative automatic thought, for example, 'This has never happened before.'	New more balanced thought, for example, 'Although I feel panicky, nothing has happened in the past and is unlikely to happen this time.'
'I'll be a laughing stock.'	My brother pointed out that my hands were shaking a couple of years back and asked me what was happening. I have thoughts about people laughing and talking about me. It's not normal for people's hands to shake.	No one was laughing. Laura still wants to go out with me. I have never seen anybody laughing ever. Most people don't care or don't notice my hands shaking. If somebody did point out that my hands were shaking it would probably say quite a lot about them, more than me.	'Yes, I do get anxious, but most people don't seem to notice or they don't care.'
'Laura is bound to have second thoughts about me.'	It took quite a while for Laura to agree to go out with me. Laura might think I'm insecure and anxious and find that unattractive.	Laura didn't mention anything. Laura's family were very friendly towards me. If Laura were to make those kind of judgements she isn't the girl I thought she was. People don't think the same way that I do. I may have other qualities that Laura likes about me.	'I do have doubts, as most teenagers do, but I've thought this several times before and nothing has happened.'

When Ben mulled over his new balanced thought he recognised that he experienced an immediate lifting of anxiety. With the help of his therapist he was able to recognise that by leaving his hands where they could be seen and focusing his attention on others he would draw far less attention to himself. After completing his NAT challenging record Ben was able to place one of his more balanced thoughts into a new positive generic cycle (see Figure 28).

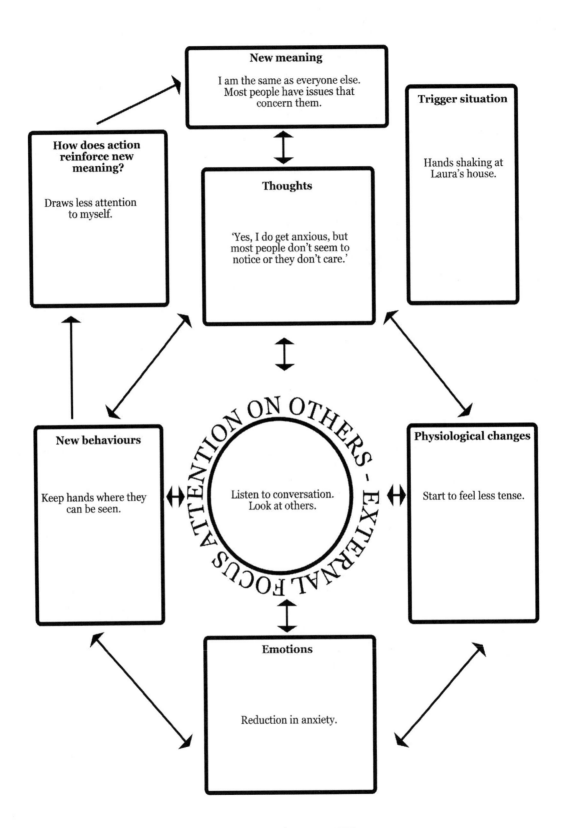

Figure 28. Ben's positive CBT cycle

79

A further example of NAT challenging

To look at NAT challenging with a slightly different anxiety issue, we will describe how NAT challenging worked with Alice. Alice thought that she was going to pass out if her symptoms did not stop. Alice's usual behaviour was to sit down and rest if she felt her symptoms coming on. This had begun to significantly hamper her life, as she felt that she could not travel and she did not want to leave her house when she felt this way. We have placed Alice's information into a generic CBT cycle adapted for panic (see Figure 29 below).

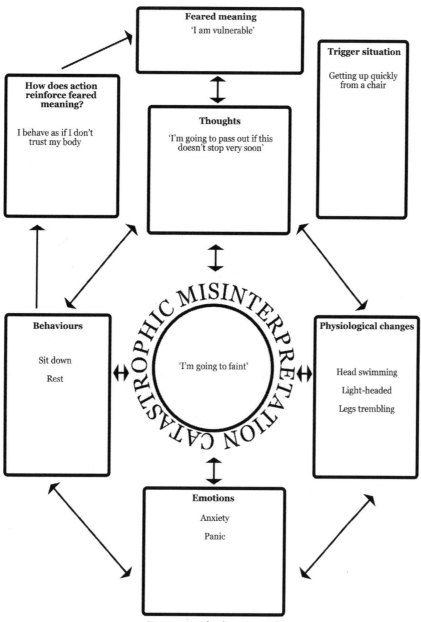

Figure 29. Alice's panic cycle

Using a NAT challenging record, Alice looked at evidence for and against her thought that she was going to pass out. With the help of her therapist, she developed a new more balanced thought (see Table 5).

Table 5. Alice's thought challenging record

Negative automatic thought, for example, 'I am going to die.'	Evidence for negative automatic thought, for example, 'I feel that it might happen.'	Evidence against negative automatic thought, for example, 'This has never happened before.'	New more balanced thought, for example, 'Although I feel panicky, nothing has happened in the past and is unlikely to happen this time.'
'I'm going to pass out if this doesn't stop very soon.'	I feel shaky. My legs feel like jelly. My mind feels like it's swimming. I feel faint.	I'm still standing. I've never passed out before. Blood pressure goes up during panic, making fainting less likely. This is just my prefrontal cortex going offline.	'My mind does feel faint and like it's swimming. It feels uncomfortable but nothing dangerous is actually happening.'

Using her new more balanced thought, Alice was able to place her new information into a positive generic cycle (see Figure 30). This then acted as a guide for Alice to start changing her behaviour.

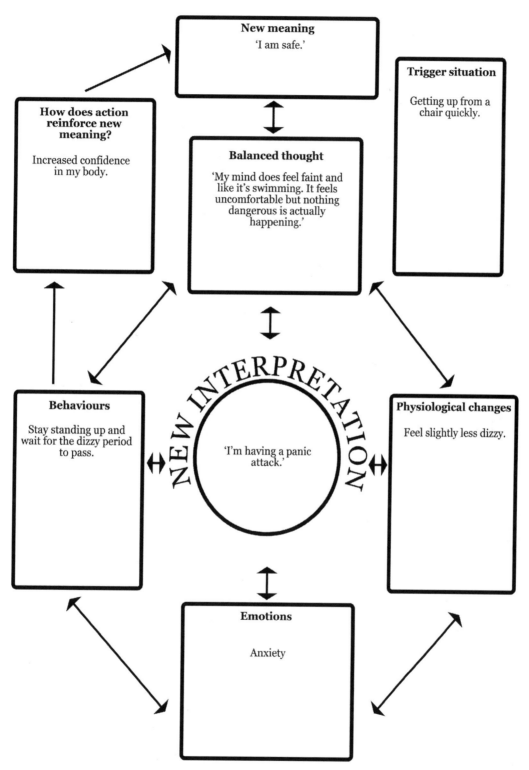

Figure 30. Alice's new positive cycle

Completing NAT challenging

Look at the diary you completed in Chapter 2 and pick out one of your NATs. Please note that it is generally best to avoid using thought challenging exercises to work with beliefs (e.g., 'I am bad', 'I am weak', 'I am a failure'). Beliefs are better challenged in a therapy environment using different types of exercises.

After you have selected a NAT, place your information into a generic CBT cycle. Then, using a thought challenging form, write down as much evidence as possible to support your NAT. Using an analogy of a prosecution lawyer and a defence lawyer in a courtroom can be very useful to generate ideas. The evidence does not have to rely on facts; for example, evidence for the NAT 'She is deliberately looking down on me' could be 'I feel that it is true', or 'I think it's true'. Only when evidence for the NAT is exhausted should you move onto the evidence against it. Drawing attention to logical facts and thinking distortions can be very useful when challenging NATs. Once evidence for and against the NAT has been identified, come up with a more balanced thought that reflects both sides of the evidence. An example of a more balanced thought could be 'I feel that she looks down on me, but in reality I don't know what she is really thinking and she is probably behaving the way that she does because she is quite shy or socially anxious'.

Once you have your new more balanced thought, place it into a positive CBT cycle and examine how this may lead to you feeling and acting differently. Your positive CBT cycle will then act as a guide for you to change your behaviour.

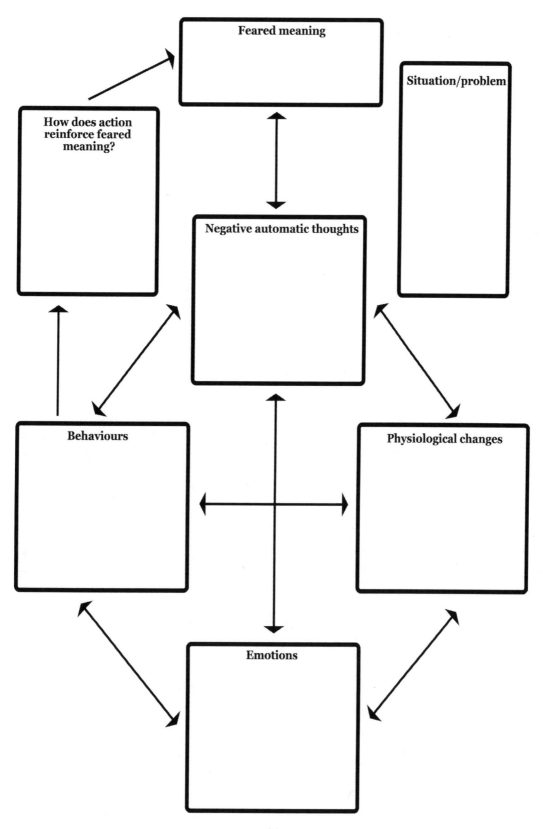

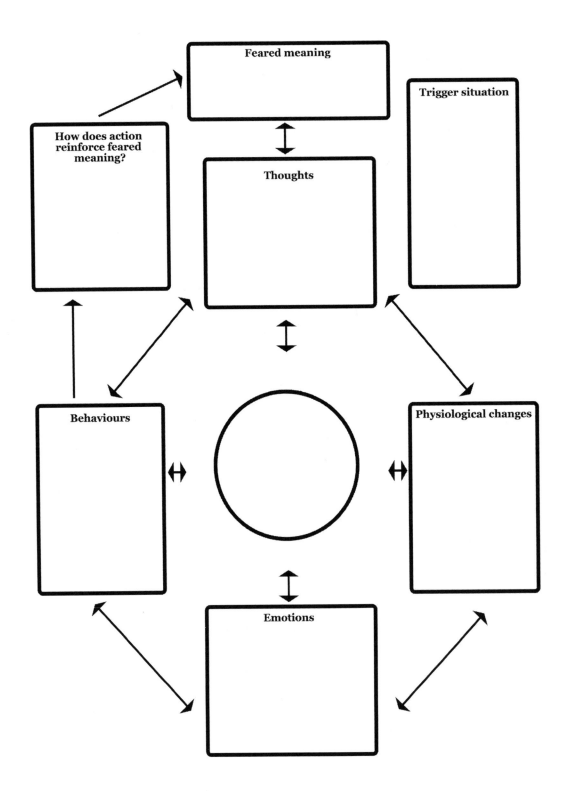

NAT challenging form

Negative automatic thought, for example, 'I am going to die.'	Evidence for negative automatic thought, for example, 'I feel that it might happen.'	Evidence against negative automatic thought, for example, 'This has never happened before.'	New more balanced thought, for example, 'Although I feel panicky, nothing has happened in the past and is unlikely to happen this time.'

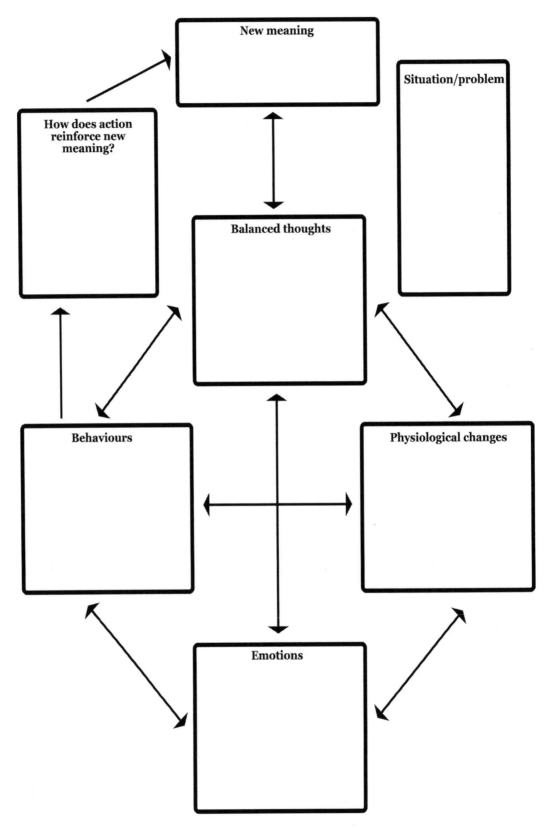

87

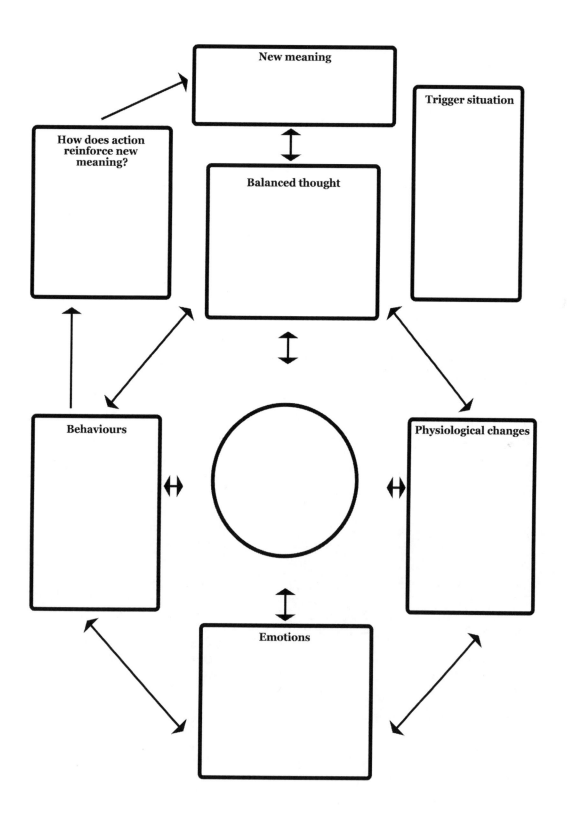

Reacting differently to thoughts

Once you recognise the types of thoughts that increase your anxiety, you have an opportunity to react differently to them. Not all thoughts need to be mulled over, believed, actioned, or dealt with, no matter how frightening or intrusive they are. Most thoughts are simply ideas or suggestions that have moved their way into conscious awareness from deeper levels of the mind. In most cases, it is our own thinking processes, mainly rumination and worry, that generate thoughts that increase anxiety.

Breaking patterns of rumination and worry

Most people who experience anxiety symptoms spend a large amount of time worrying or ruminating. Processes of rumination and worry are kept in place by the questions we ask ourselves. For example, if we ask, 'Why does this keep happening to me?' or 'What's wrong with me?' these questions will simply throw up answers that, in turn, can lead us to ask more questions. Before long, if this process continues unstopped we can end up confirming our worst fears – for example, that we are in danger, worthless, weak, wrong, useless, bad, and such like. The irony of the whole process is that in our search for ways to avoid current or future painful feelings by ruminating or worrying we end up dwelling on our thoughts and we feel worse than ever. It's not dissimilar to using a shovel to dig ourselves out of a hole. The more we dig, the deeper the hole gets! The problem is that often we do not feel that we have any other way of solving our problems, so we continue to use the same strategy, even though we know it does not work. To demonstrate we will offer you a hypothetical discussion between a CBT therapist and a client.

CLIENT: What's the difference between worry and rumination?

CBT THERAPIST: Worry and rumination are similar in that they both involve thought churning. The main difference between them is that worry is focused on the future and being able to cope with potential outcomes, whereas rumination is focused on the past.

When people worry, they think about upcoming situations and ask questions such as, 'What will I do if…?'; 'What is the worst thing that could happen?' or 'What if this happens?' They do this because they think that if they can imagine the worst-case scenario, then they will be able to put things in place to deal with whatever happens in a particular situation. They think if they can work out what might happen in advance, then they will be safe. Ironically, however, just like rumination, in an attempt to achieve certainty and to feel safe, we can end up feeling more frightened than ever, and also experience intrusive thoughts.

CLIENT: Intrusive thoughts?

CBT THERAPIST: An intrusive thought is a thought that pushes its way into awareness with extreme urgency. Intrusive thoughts often appear to come out of nowhere and carry high levels of emotional distress with them.

Before I explain why intrusive thoughts may occur, I want to offer you a simple analogy about the mind's functioning.

First I'd like you to recognise that people have a conscious mind. When people use their conscious minds they are awake to thoughts, images, or sensations that they experience. I'd like us to imagine that the conscious mind is a bit like a magic whiteboard that begins to erase what is written on it after only a few seconds. Because the ink or information expressed using the ink disappears so rapidly, the only way to keep anything live on this whiteboard is to continuously write on it over and over again. When new information is written on the whiteboard, information that was on the whiteboard previously disappears even more rapidly. A further point to note is that the amount of information that can be written on the whiteboard at any one point in time is limited due to the whiteboard's small size.

CLIENT: So you are saying the mind is like a whiteboard? I'm not sure I understand what you mean?

CBT THERAPIST: Do you mind if I demonstrate with you? It's much easier to show you how this works rather than to explain it. Before we start I just want to let you know that this is not a test. It's just a little exercise so that you can find out how much information your mind can hold onto. I am going to start by asking you to remember five random numbers and letters. Are you ready?

CLIENT: Yes.

CBT THERAPIST: 5A3KQ. Have you got that?

CLIENT: Yes. I think so!

CBT THERAPIST: Alright, I now want you to remember these numbers as well.

27KR1…Right, can you repeat that sequence for me?

CLIENT: 27KR1.

CBT THERAPIST: Good…And, the first sequence?

CLIENT: …Erm … [a big pause follows] …57…Q…It seems to have gone out of my head… I'm sorry.

CBT THERAPIST: There's no need to be sorry. This is exactly what is meant to happen. This is how the mind works. We just gave your internal whiteboard an impossible task. Hardly anyone can recall over nine randomly presented units of information unless they use specialised memory techniques, and I just gave you ten. That's why I'm saying the whiteboard is small.

I'll just explain it a bit more. A benefit of the whiteboard's disappearing ink process is that it is constantly available for continuous use. As a result of this, huge amounts of information can be written on the whiteboard during the period of its lifetime. In many respects, it could be suggested that we should feel grateful that the whiteboard loses access to information so quickly. If it didn't it would quite quickly become jammed up with too much information and become unusable.

Taking this idea further, I'd like us to imagine that our out-of-conscious processes work a little like a building that the whiteboard is housed in. I'll just explain that out-of-conscious processes are brain functions that we are unaware of, or mental processes that go on in the back of our minds.

CLIENT: And what's the significance of associating the out-of-conscious mind with a building?

CBT THERAPIST: I'm saying that out-of-conscious processes are like a building because the amount of brain space required for out-of-conscious thinking is absolutely huge in comparison to the amount of brain space used for the whiteboard. The building is also three-dimensional, unlike the two-dimensional whiteboard. There are also multiple rooms, and secret passageways.

CLIENT: I understand why it is big but what does the three-dimensional layout of the building represent, with multiple rooms and such like?

CBT THERAPIST: This represents an idea that the out-of-conscious mind can think on several different levels at the same time. It can absorb information from our environment, take care of all of our bodily functions, plan our activities, assist our communication, and think about problems we have in our lives without us being aware it is happening. It can also use symbols, images, and words to create ideas and connect them up in a way that we would struggle to do consciously. What it can do is really quite incredible!

In this building there are also filing cabinets crammed with information that we thought we had forgotten about, and there are reams of papers lying around waiting to be filed.

CLIENT: What do the reams of papers represent?

CBT THERAPIST: The reams of paper represent thoughts that we have not fully processed or ideas that we are currently working on. Many people may have several hundred or even thousands of different thought strands they are working on at any one time. Thought strands may be about relationships with different people, hobbies or interests, work projects, holidays and such like. Information does not disappear easily from this building but very often it can get lost or misfiled.

CLIENT: So how does it get lost or misfiled?

CBT THERAPIST: There is so much information in this building or in people's minds that sometimes it is hard for them to find what they are looking for. The more information that's in the building the harder it is to find what is needed.

Now imagine that in this building there is a librarian who is very loyal to you and will try to find answers to anything that you ask using the whiteboard, even if it means working through the night. Sometimes the librarian finds information quickly, sometimes it might take days, but when the librarian finds answers to questions posed on the whiteboard she will post an answer on the whiteboard just as soon as space becomes available.

CLIENT: I'm still not sure I fully understand this analogy of a librarian. How does this work with real problems?

CBT THERAPIST: OK. Let's imagine that you are walking down the street one day and on the other side of the street there is a girl whose face you recognise. You are immediately aware that you know her but this is not where you usually see her. You ask yourself 'Where do I know her from?' a few times. Nothing comes to mind immediately and you carry on doing whatever you were doing before. You may even forget that you asked that question as it disappears from your conscious awareness and is replaced by other things. However, a little while later, maybe a few hours, days, or sometimes weeks later, an idea pops into your mind telling you where you knew the person you saw in the street from. How do you think this might happen?

CLIENT: Well, I guess the librarian had not forgotten that I asked that question; perhaps she was going through the filing cabinets looking for an answer, or maybe she waited for me to go somewhere and suddenly remembered.

CBT THERAPIST: That's what I'm saying. As soon as an opportunity occurred, and there was space available on the whiteboard, the librarian posted the information. A useful rule of thumb, therefore, will be to assume that when we ask our brain questions it will continue to work on questions posed to it even though we may have consciously forgotten that we have asked the questions in the first place.

Usually the librarian will put thoughts or information in a queue to enter conscious awareness, and in this respect answers to questions you have asked will wait patiently to pop into your mind when there is space available or when the mind is not occupied with something else.

CLIENT: Is that why so many thoughts go through my head at night just as I want to go to sleep?

CBT THERAPIST: Yes, that's what I'm getting at. You will have access to these thoughts at night because your mind is not focused on other things.

CLIENT: What about the other thoughts you mentioned earlier? I think you said they were intrusive thoughts. I used to get those a lot?

CBT THERAPIST: Intrusive thoughts are different to the above-mentioned thoughts that we have. They are not dissimilar to the librarian pushing through a registered letter for your attention. Intrusive thoughts are pushed through to consciousness, as a priority, pushing out any other information that is currently online. You may be talking with someone when one of these thoughts pops into your head. For example, if you are socially anxious, an image of yourself looking odd could suddenly be pushed into your mind. Intrusive thoughts are sent with high degrees of importance and you will notice them as a result of the high levels of emotional intensity that come with them.

CLIENT: So where do they come from?

CBT THERAPIST: There may be many factors responsible for the creation of intrusive thoughts. One way that they may be generated is by worrying or asking 'What if?' questions. This type of questioning process certainly appears to increase the likelihood of intrusive thoughts being pushed into consciousness. It is important to recognise that when we receive intrusive thought messages they are not 'evidence' for anything. Although intrusive thoughts often feel uncomfortable, because they bring fear with them, it does not make these thoughts any more real than any other thoughts that pop into your mind.

I think the best way to explain this is by talking about a young man I worked with a little while ago.

Gregory was a big worrier. He would often go through a process of worry, asking 'What if?' questions to his mind and his brain would usually send him back the worst possible things that could happen, or what could go wrong. His intentions for worrying were positive, as he felt that this type of questioning process could keep him safe. He thought that if he knew about the types of problems that might occur in advance then he could be prepared for them. Before going to the cinema with friends, Gregory would ask himself about what could go wrong. His obedient mind usually sent him answers. One type of answer generated and sent to his conscious awareness was that he might end up in a middle seat feeling panicky, with everyone around noticing him, and he would feel humiliated.

CLIENT: I think most people would be anxious about that, wouldn't they?

CBT THERAPIST: They might do if they worried a lot about what people thought about them. But remember, nothing had actually happened at this point. This was all in his mind. But, based on the ideas that his mind gave him, Gregory decided to take action and sit at the back near an aisle seat so that he could make a quick exit if required. Gregory then began to think of how he could position himself in an aisle seat. He thought that if he could go in first in his group of friends, he could stand near an aisle seat and gesture to the others to go in ahead of him. His mind came up with further ideas, such as, if anyone questioned his need to sit in an aisle seat, he would say that he had a stomach ache and might need to go to the bathroom. He also had thoughts about phoning his friends up at the last minute and telling them that he couldn't make it. The amount of worrying that Gregory experienced before going to the cinema made the whole process of going to the cinema a difficult experience rather than the enjoyable one that it could have been. Gregory's mind also reminded him how strange he was for engaging in this type of behaviour, and his friends would never think that he was like that.

CLIENT: So what happened to him?

CBT THERAPIST: A big risk for Gregory was deciding not to ask 'What if?' questions. Gregory thought that asking himself these questions kept him prepared, safe and not vulnerable. Recognising that all thoughts that come into awareness are simply offerings sent by the mind and not ideas supported by evidence made a significant difference to Gregory. Gregory learnt how to stand back and observe his thoughts, and recognise that any thought that came into awareness was just a suggestion. Just because he had a thought it did not mean it needed to be dealt with immediately. As such, learning to notice his thoughts made a significant difference to him.

Many people's minds come up with all sorts of negative ideas when they worry. In Gregory's case, a worry for him was losing control, being thought of as weak by others, and others thinking that there was something wrong with him. I drew a diagram on my office whiteboard for Gregory to look at. I have copied it for you to look at. (See Figure 31.)

Gregory carried out numerous avoidant-type behaviours that tended to confirm his fear-based thoughts still further. By carrying out avoidant behaviours, Gregory didn't collect alternative accurate evidence that he could use to challenge his fears.

Gregory's example shows how the interactions between thoughts, feelings, and behaviour have a tendency to maintain problems. In this case, interrupting Gregory's worry processes led to him having fewer frightening thoughts, which in turn led to a reduction in his tendency to want to avoid situations.

Research

Intrusive thoughts are defined as unwanted thoughts, images, or impulses. In 2014, Richard Moulding and his colleagues completed an international study to identify a) the prevalence of intrusive thoughts and b) how people react to them. They assessed 777 students across 15 cities, 13 countries, and 6 continents. They found that 93% of their students had experienced intrusive thoughts in the previous three months, suggesting that intrusive thoughts are in fact a normal part of daily living. The researchers' natural conclusion was therefore: It is not the intrusive thoughts themselves that maintain mental health problems, but rather how we react to them.

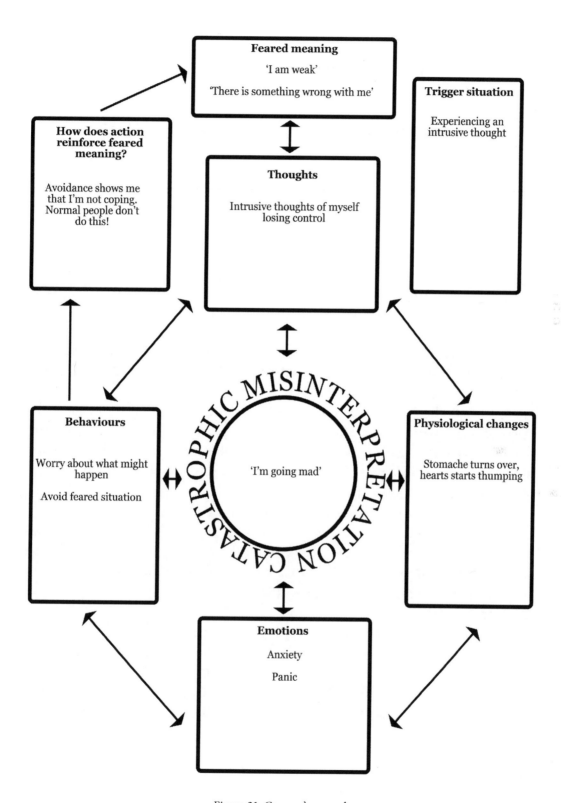

Figure 31. Gregory's example

CHAPTER 10

Learn how to interact with feelings in a different way

Melissa B., a teacher, was sitting in front of her therapist. As she spoke, she shifted around continuously in her chair, rubbing the back of her neck, grabbing her long red hair, breathing from the top of her chest, sighing and holding her breath at various times. She appeared to be a highly analytical person and was able to articulate her difficulties quite easily. She explained how interpersonal difficulties between herself and work colleagues had started, and she had insight into these problems. However, when she was asked how she was feeling in her body, she found it extremely difficult to answer. It wasn't the case that Melissa didn't experience emotions, as she was displaying them quite evidently in front of her therapist, through her body language. It was more a case that Melissa felt very uncomfortable when she recognised her bodily sensations of anxiety and felt a lot more familiar remaining or staying put in her head. When Melissa was asked if she had ever developed any positive coping strategies to soothe herself she couldn't think of any. She stated quite simply that she had been brought up in a household where people didn't talk about their feelings. As a result of this, from a very early age Melissa had naturally developed many sophisticated ways of ignoring or controlling her emotions and in fact had become quite an expert in emotional avoidance.

Figure 32 shows an example of the type of relationship that many individuals with anxiety have with their feelings. Generally, painful emotions such as anxiety, as well as anger and sadness, are viewed as feelings to be feared or to be got rid of. As a result, strategies such as ignoring feelings, distracting the self from feeling feelings, and using safety behaviours to avoid feelings are commonly used. People's natural instinct is to suppress uncomfortable feelings in order to feel better. However, an unfortunate consequence of engaging in emotionally avoidant strategies is that emotional distress is maintained at quite a high level or it increases even further over time.

A counter-intuitive solution to anxiety

The ideas covered in the right-hand column of Table 6 (see below, right) often confuse many people because the concepts feel so alien to them. Maybe it's not dissimilar to asking them to grab a red-hot poker, while assuring them that it is not going to harm them. This type of counter-intuitive strategy to anxiety is the last thing that most people who experience anxiety would choose to do as they feel that their anxiety will rise significantly. By the way, when we say 'counter-intuitive' we mean people carrying out behaviours or engaging in thoughts that are the direct opposite of what their intuition or feelings tell them is right.

What would happen if you tried the opposite of the above? For example, instead of ignoring emotions, you notice them and tell them that it is fine for them to be there?

What if instead of distracting yourself from anxiety, you focus on your feelings, and spend time in your body rather than in your head?

What would happen if you began to see anxiety as a friend rather than your enemy, if you allow your anxiety to be visible rather than try to hide it, and give permission for your anxiety to stay, rather than trying to get rid of it as soon as possible?

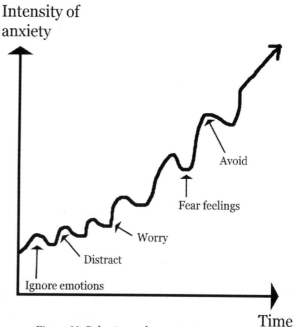

Figure 32. Behaviours that maintain anxiety

Table 6. A new approach to feelings

Commonly applied solutions to anxiety	Strategy based on an opposites approach
Avoid uncomfortable feelings.	Approach uncomfortable feelings.
Distract self. Keep mind off feelings.	Focus on feelings.
Perceive anxiety symptoms as threatening. Fear them.	Perceive anxiety as part of the body that works for you. Embrace symptoms and allow symptoms to be visible.
Control anxiety, try to get rid of feelings as soon as possible.	Allow anxiety to freely move about body.
Tell anxiety that it shouldn't be there.	Tell anxiety that it is OK to be there and it can stay as long as it wants.

96

An effective way to approach accepting feelings

If you remind yourself of the ideas covered in the early part of this book, you will remember that the neocortex is at the top of the brain, the prefrontal cortex is directly next to it, and the subcortical regions are at the bottom of the brain. A slight problem with people who become highly anxious and panicky is that their prefrontal cortex tends to go offline when they are feeling most distressed. If this happens to you, you could find yourself in situations when you are panicking, with your mind going blank, finding it very difficult to think clearly or rationally, and feeling unable to complete CBT exercises.

With this in mind, we suggest that a very useful starting point will be to begin viewing yourself as a parent to the subcortical or primitive regions of the brain. Imagine these parts of the brain not as the enemy, but more like a servant who has worked for you loyally and tirelessly; a servant who is also very rarely appreciated for his or her efforts in assisting you.

'I've got a niggling feeling that Madam's not
very happy with me'

The best place to start your new parenting approach will be when you are on your own and when your anxiety levels are mild. Mild anxiety may be around when you have day-to-day problems; for example, a problem at work, a problem with a friend or a relative etc. Mild distress may also be around when you worry, or when you ask 'What if?' questions. The essence of the approach that we are going to suggest you use is to become more aware of your feelings, especially anxious feelings, at the earliest stage possible. The best way to explain is with a demonstration. This is how a conversation with a client might develop.

CBT THERAPIST: OK, Jemma, I would just like you to think of a problem that you have had just recently; a problem that when you think about it now, still leaves you feeling slightly anxious.

JEMMA: OK, I've thought of something. Do you want me to talk to you about it?

CBT THERAPIST: No, I'd like you to keep it to yourself for now. I'd just like you to think about where you feel your emotions more strongly.

JEMMA: I feel it most in my chest!

CBT THERAPIST: Good. Keep your focus there. Now place one of your hands on your chest in the place where you feel your emotion more strongly. You are placing your hand on your body where your emotion is, because many of us who are prone to avoiding emotions unconsciously and automatically move away from feeling emotions, and go into our heads instead. You are gaining a connection with your emotions and keeping your focus on how you are feeling.

Placing your hand on the part of your body where you feel your anxiety more strongly will also act as a reminder to you to keep your focus on your emotions. It is very important while you are doing this exercise to focus on feeling your feelings and remind yourself that you really are willing for your emotions to be there. Focusing your mind on the part of your body underneath your hand, examine exactly what your emotion feels like. For example, how much space do your feelings take up? How painful or uncomfortable are your feelings. Jemma, can you rate the intensity of your feeling between 1 and 10, where 10 is the highest level of intensity? The threat does not need to be valid in the current time mode. If it has been perceived as a threat in the past, or you have previously confirmed the existence of the threat by withdrawing from this threat in the past, then from the primitive mind's point of view the threat is still active.

While feeling your symptoms of anxiety, it is important when you speak to your feelings that you really mean what you are saying. Let go of all your thoughts and focus on your feeling. The importance of your self-communication is not in the words that you use but rather your intention behind your words. Keep an idea in mind of accepting, recognising, being grateful, and being patient. I'm just going to ask you to do this for a minute, Jemma, and we will see what happens.

[…a minute passes…]

CBT THERAPIST: What are you noticing at the moment, Jemma?

JEMMA: The feeling is going down…It's about a 4 now.

CBT THERAPIST: OK keep with the feeling, noticing that it is going down. Just stay with it. We'll see what ,happens in another minute or so.

[…another minute passes…]

CBT THERAPIST: OK, Jemma what are you noticing now?

JEMMA: It's gone!

Learning how to stay with your feelings

It is important in the early stages of this approach that you practise being with your feelings as much as possible. This will help you in two ways. Firstly, it will help you to fear your feelings less; secondly it will make it more likely that you will be able to use your acceptance approach when you are experiencing higher levels of anxiety. You will need to bear in mind that in a state of heightened distress the frontal lobes – where your self-soothing approach comes from – stop working somewhat. Practising acceptance over and over again when you are not so anxious will make it more likely that you will be able to access and use this self-soothing approach automatically when you need it the most.

The basal ganglia kicks in when we feel distressed

When we become highly anxious, we are likely to continue to return to our old unhelpful habitual behaviours due to the strong influence of a part of the brain called the basal ganglia, which is located in the subcortical region of the brain. Activation of the basal ganglia results in us doing the same things that we have always done before. To change the use of unhelpful habits, you will need to practise using your new positive habits – learned through CBT exercises – over and over again. Eventually, your new CBT habits will come into place automatically when you are faced with distressing situations. This process takes time, however, as brain wiring in the basal ganglia does not grow instantly.

CHAPTER 11

Altering the body's physiological processes to break cycles of anxiety

There are several ways to change physiological processes associated with anxiety and we will describe several strategies in this chapter. It is important to note that these strategies are not designed to encourage avoidance of symptoms of anxiety. (Avoidance is likely to result in your anxiety symptoms remaining for a longer period of time.)

Temporarily reduce your stress levels

Individuals with stressful lives can experience high baseline anxiety/stress levels due to a number of factors. Based on this suggestion, it could be helpful for you to look at specific areas where you may be able to temporarily reduce your stress levels, thereby reducing your overall threat response activation. Solutions for stress reduction could be a) working fewer hours, or b) lessening commitments in various areas. Reducing stress levels will not necessarily remove anxiety symptoms, but it can lead to symptoms becoming less severe.

Abdominal breathing

One strategy to utilise if you are experiencing panic symptoms is abdominal breathing. Deliberately breathe deeply and slowly, inhaling air to the bottom of your lungs while concentrating on your breath. This will help to prevent hyper-ventilation, one of the main reasons for an experience of dizziness or light-headedness. If you are experiencing panic symptoms, breathing more slowly will reduce the amount of carbon dioxide that is leaving your body, producing a calming effect.

Focused distraction

A temporary short-term strategy for anxiety is focused distraction. Distraction can be used to prevent negative self-talk and catastrophic thinking. There are a number of different ways of carrying out distraction. One method is to look at the details of everything around you, focusing your attention externally. In this respect you will be looking at the colours, textures, smells, and patterns in your surroundings. This is deliberate behaviour designed to intentionally divert your focus away from frightening thoughts and feelings, and towards an awareness of your environment. When you do this, ask yourself, 'What do I see, hear, or notice outside of myself?'

Guided imagery

Guided imagery can reduce anxiety symptoms for many people. As a result of being offered imaginary information through the senses, the primitive part of the mind can be deceived into believing that he or she is in an imaginary place, thereby creating a calming effect. When primitive areas of the brain become calmer, this then allows the regulator (prefrontal cortex) and thinking mind (neocortex) to become more dominant. At times, guided imagery is sufficient to break many individuals out of an anxious state, which in turn helps people to gain access to more balanced thoughts. Guided imagery exercises can be downloaded from the internet or purchased as digital downloads/CDs. The best imagery exercises focus on all of the senses, particularly what is seen, heard, and felt. We have placed a typical imagery exercise at the end of this chapter, called the Safe place exercise (see Tables 7a and 7b).

Systematic relaxation

One strategy to utilise if you are experiencing panic symptoms is systematic relaxation. This can be achieved by focusing on one area of the body at a time, and by either clenching or stretching muscles. Most systematic relaxation exercises start with the toes and gradually work through the body until finally reaching the head. As with guided imagery, these exercises can easily be downloaded from the internet or purchased as digital downloads or as CDs. Yoga helps many people with anxiety and it incorporates many of these exercises.

Exercise

Some studies have found that regular exercise produces the same benefits to mood as medication, while other studies have found that people who carry out regular exercise have better mental health than those who do not. Many experts suggest that exercise improves mood by reducing stress levels: several scientific studies have found that although levels of cortisol - a hormone associated with stress - increase during exercise, cortisol levels after exercise become lower and remain at more balanced levels.

Massage

Several studies have found that massage (involving skin-to-skin touch) reduces anxiety and stress levels. The type of massage does not seem to matter. Interestingly, massages, in which massage therapists wore gloves, instead of using skin on skin contact, were not found to be as effective at relieving anxiety.

Medication

Medication is still the most commonly used treatment for anxiety, and evidence indicates that a combination of CBT and medication is more beneficial than using either approach alone. There are logical reasons that explain why medication enhances a CBT approach. If, at an organic level, the mind does not have the capacity to think straight, there is very little likelihood that people will have the concentration or energy to complete CBT exercises effectively, or to make any of the changes we have covered in this book. Medication may give people the extra energy or boost required to make these changes. Equally, if you take medication without making any changes to your behaviour you will not be making the best use of your medication.

Mindfulness

Growing evidence indicates that mindfulness can be very helpful for people who experience anxiety. Mindfulness encourages the processing and observation of feelings; helps people to stay in the present moment and detach themselves from rumination and worry and; exercises the prefrontal cortex, which then becomes more effective at 1) reducing background noise in the mind, and 2) regulating emotions.

As with the use of CBT exercises, you will need to keep using mindfulness-based approaches in order to maintain your positive mood state. Being mindful will also help you become much more aware of the types of environment and people that impact on your mood state. With awareness comes choice. You can choose to move away from negative environments and negative people if you wish. Equally, you can choose to think negatively about others or you can choose to think compassionately.

A mindfulness practice can be incorporated into many daily activities to make good use of your time. You can use a mindfulness practice in the shower, while eating, running, driving, and doing housework. The list is endless. A mindfulness practice does not necessarily need additional time once you have taken the time to learn how to complete the exercises.

Eye Movement Desensitisation and Reprocessing (EMDR)

EMDR is best known for its use with individuals suffering from Post-Traumatic Stress Disorder. Rapid eye movement is used in conjunction with accessing traumas, which allows people to process partially processed or unprocessed memories. As unprocessed memories are stored in subcortical regions of the brain, there is a tendency for many individuals to become emotionally distressed in environments that have cues connected to their previous memories. When this occurs, people can feel emotionally distressed, but will often not understand why.

EMDR reduces the impact of traumatic memories on anxiety and many people find that after they have had a course of EMDR their anxiety has been turned down a notch or two.

Walking in the woods

Although walking in the woods could be classed as exercise (which we have already covered), many scientists suggest that additional benefits beyond exercise can be obtained by breathing in phytoncides emitted by plants. Plants emit phytoncides to protect themselves from rotting and being eaten by insects. Breathing in phytoncides is thought to enhance immune system functioning in humans.

Cold showers

This is perhaps the quickest but also most uncomfortable way to change physiological state among the ideas we have included in this chapter. Cold showers trigger a process known as vasoconstriction. This results in blood being pushed away from the extremities and moved towards the core. Research has found that cold showers reduce levels of cortisol in the body. If you are considering having cold showers it is best to introduce your body to the shower gradually, for example putting one part of your body in cold water first, before immersing the whole body.

Cut back on caffeine

A huge number of scientific studies have found that consuming caffeinated products, such as cola, tea, and coffee, increase anxiety levels. For some, high levels of caffeine consumption can lead to panic attacks.

Reduce alcohol consumption

Although many people find that drinking alcohol helps them to relax, relaxation only occurs in the initial phase. As the body works to metabolise or burn off alcohol, anxiety actually increases. As a result, many people with anxiety notice they wake up feeling more anxious when they have consumed alcohol the night before.

Table 7a. Safe place exercise

Safe place exercise – Page 1

Think of a place where you can go on your own. Ideally a place not connected with friends or relatives. An outdoor place where you feel safe and relaxed. Write down a brief description of your place below.

Park. Walking down a wood chip path, surrounded by trees.

Look ahead and notice the details of what you see. Write down what you see here. In particular, notice the details of what you see.

I can see a small piece of tree trunk. I can see the mud of the path with wood chip in some places. I can see the path ahead with several different varieties of trees. I can see nettles and wild flowers growing.

Look to your left and write down what you see. In particular, notice the details of what you see.

To my left I can see a path veering towards the field. As I look through the trees I can make out a meandering river.

Look to your right and write down what you see. In particular, notice the details of what you see.

To my right I can see weeds, small shrubs and more trees. I can see a short wooden fence, a drainage bank, and then I can see a road in the distance.

Listen to the sounds that you hear. What do you notice?

I can hear a faint sound of rustling leaves. Maybe a slight vibration of traffic on a nearby road.

How do you feel when you hear these sounds?
Calm and relaxed.

Breathe in. What sensations do you notice in terms of how your breath feels? What does this place smell like?

I notice the air is fresh. There is a slight musty smell from warm wood chips baking in the sun.

Safe place exercise – Page 2

Become aware of the air against your skin. What tells you from what you feel on your skin that you are in this place?

Cool all over. Mainly on my face and on my hands.

Feel the ground underneath your feet. What sensations do you notice?

The ground is slightly bouncy from the wood chips and gives a little because of the wet earth.

Bring to awareness what you see, what you hear, the sensations on your skin, the feeling of the ground underneath your feet. How do you feel?

Calm, relaxed, and still.

If there was a word that decribes how this place makes you feel, what would that word be?

Safe.

**Repeat your word in your mind while you remain in your safe place.
What do you notice?**

A relaxed, tingling feeling in my body.

What do you notice happening in your body while you are in your safe place?
Feeling clam and a little sleepy.

Safe place exercise – Page 1

Think of a place where you can go on your own. Ideally a place not connected with friends or relatives. An outdoor place where you feel safe and relaxed. Write down a brief description of your place below.

Look ahead and notice the details of what you see. Write down what you see here. In particular, notice the details of what you see.

Look to your left and write down what you see. In particular, notice the details of what you see.

Look to your right and write down what you see. In particular, notice the details of what you see.

Listen to the sounds that you hear. What do you notice?

How do you feel when you hear these sounds?

Breathe in. What sensations to you notice in terms of how your breath feels? What does this place smell like?

Become aware of the air against your skin. What tells you from what you feel on your skin that you are in this place?

Feel the ground underneath your feet. What sensations do you notice?

Bring to awareness what you see, what you hear, the sensations on your skin, the feeling of the ground underneath your feet. How do you feel?

If there was a word that decribes how this place makes you feel, what would that word be?

Repeat your word in your mind while you remain in your safe place.
What do you notice?

What do you notice happening in your body while you are in your safe place?

CHAPTER 12

Break anxiety cycles by changing behaviour

Y ou may well have read the contents of this book and hopefully by now have more knowledge about anxiety. However, despite this, you may continue to experience intense feelings of anxiety in various situations. If you are at this stage, your thinking mind understands anxiety, but the primitive part of your brain has yet to take on board the same information.

With this in mind, one of the most helpful ways to teach the primitive mind how to absorb new information is through experience. We will explain using an analogy.

We would like to invite you to think of the primitive mind as a child who comes to your bedroom door one night feeling frightened. You ask the child what she is frightened of and she says that she thinks there is something – a monster – in her wardrobe. You have several options in terms of your potential responses.

- You could tell the child not to be so silly and completely ignore her. The result of this is that the child waits around outside your room and continues to try to gain your attention. She could even wait outside your bedroom door for the whole night.

- You could rationalise with the child. You explain to her how impossible it is that a monster could get into her wardrobe and that monsters don't exist. You tell her that she is thinking about monsters because she watched a frightening television programme about monsters earlier. The result of this is that the child nods while listening and goes back to her room for a short while, but is back outside your room a few minutes later.

- You could tell the child that she can sleep in a put-down bed in your room. The child is not scared anymore and happily gets into this bed. However, when the next day comes she seems more terrified than before of sleeping in her bedroom.

Or

- You could take the child's hand, acknowledging that she feels really frightened, and tell her that you are both going to look into the wardrobe together. When you approach the wardrobe, the child is really scared and she tries to resist going towards the wardrobe. You gently persist, telling the child that it really is OK to feel frightened. When you have opened the wardrobe door and you both have had a good look inside for a couple of minutes, you notice that the child has become a lot less anxious and is happier once more to sleep in her own bed.

With the last option, you don't have to explain or rationalise; you simply help the child to acknowledge that she is scared. You take her to the situation that you know logically is very low risk (i.e., there is a very low probability of there actually being a monster in her wardrobe) and encourage her to find out for herself how dangerous the situation is. The child learns by her own experience.

Behavioural experiments

Behavioural experiments can be very helpful in challenging thoughts that drive anxiety. The general idea behind them is to teach the self to learn positive behaviour change through breaking patterns of old unhelpful behaviour. To carry out a behavioural experiment, you will need to make a decision to change a behaviour and then put yourself directly in a position to make that behaviour change happen. You will need to make a prediction before the behaviour is carried out (what you think or feel might happen). When you carry out the behaviour, it is important that you record the results. The majority of us make assumptions about: a) how others might react to our behaviour, or b) how we might feel if we carry out a certain behaviour. A lot of the time, however, our assumptions are based on inaccurate information or indeed a lack of knowledge. Behavioural experiments help with the development of experiential knowledge.

Completing a behavioural experiment will involve you making a prediction about what you think may occur if you change your behaviour in a particular situation. After you have made a prediction, you will then carry out your new behaviour and observe what occurs. We have made lists of potential behavioural experiments that can be carried out on pages 115 to 120.

CBT therapists regularly carry out behavioural experiments with their clients. Typically, behavioural experiments can be used to challenge catastrophic misinterpretations, such as: 'I'm going to faint'; 'I'm going to fall over'; 'I'm going to lose control'; 'People are going to laugh at me' etc.

Setting up behavioural experiments

To give you an idea about how this might work, we will describe the case of Jenny who had social anxiety. Jenny was a fair-haired, university researcher in her early thirties. She was a highly intelligent woman with a doctorate in physics. In early sessions with her therapist it appeared as though she could barely move in her chair. When she was asked what had brought her to therapy, it seemed that this question was deeply painful for her. She was unable to offer any reply apart from 'I'm not sure' or 'I don't know'. She appeared deeply embarrassed by her inability to respond more fully to her therapist's questions. More than a minute at a time would pass before Jenny offered even the most simple of responses.

After a while, Jenny's therapist discovered that Jenny was carrying out a process of self-monitoring, and assessing everything that she might say. Jenny said that she often did this at work and in particular when she was required to deliver lectures. The thought of presenting lectures filled Jenny with dread for weeks or months in advance. Jenny spent enormous amounts of time preparing for her lectures, and rehearsing possible question-and-answer scenarios. In fact, she reported that her stress levels were so high that on some occasions she had been ready to hand in her resignation, but then later changed her mind.

Jenny reported that when faced with unavoidable social situations she had developed a number of coping strategies. Jenny had a fear of her mind going blank when she was anxious and didn't trust what she might say in these situations. As a result of this she would spend time repeating what she wanted to say over and over in her mind before saying anything. On some occasions, she repeated what she was going to say in her mind so many times that she forgot what was being discussed, which led to her feeling highly embarrassed. Saying what was in her mind felt like a risk and she felt she could reduce the risk if she said as little as possible.

Jenny had gone to quite extreme lengths to hide her symptoms from others. Her predominant behaviour pattern was avoidance. Although her university department regularly organised social events for the staff, she managed to avoid all of them by offering a variety of plausible excuses. Jenny was meticulous with her job, putting in lots of extra time to produce work of a very high standard, and she was highly appreciated by her university colleagues.

Jenny and her therapist drew up a list of potential behaviour changes with an idea that she would start with changing behaviours that produced lower levels of anxiety first (see Table 8). One of Jenny's behavioural experiments is shown using Table 9.

Table 8. Jenny's list

Potential behaviours to challenge

Feared situation or feared behaviour	What do I fear might happen?	Anxiety Rate out of 10 where 10 is the maximum
Reduce lecture preparation time to the same as other academics.	People will find out that I am not really up to the job and that I am a fraud.	9
Speak without thinking through exactly what I am going to say.	I will say something stupid and embarrass myself.	8
Focus on others instead of myself.	Dropping my guard will end up with me saying something stupid.	4
Allow my anxiety to be there.	My anxiety might take me by surprise and others might notice.	2
Say what I think a bit more in social situations.	People might judge me or think that I am stupid.	6
Stand in the foreground in social situations.	I will draw more attention to myself and will look awkward and uncomfortable.	5
Arrive early to social events.	I will feel uncomfortable and awkward and will have to make conversation with people.	5
Suspend worrying. Deal with things when and if they happen.	I will be unprepared and will flounder.	5

Potential behaviours to challenge

Feared situation or feared behaviour	What do I fear might happen?	Anxiety Rate out of 10 where 10 is the maximum

Table 9. Jenny's behavioural experiment

Behavioural experiment sheet

Describe old behaviour or safety behaviour

Focus on myself to see how I am coming across.

Describe new behaviour

Focus externally.

How will you carry out new behaviour?

When I am in a social situation I will place my attention as much as possible on the other person. I will look at the other person and I will listen to what he or she has to say. If my mind turns inward to looking at myself I will spot this and without judging myself I will immediately shift my attention towards focusing externally.

Predictions about what will happen when you drop the safety behaviour. Write down as many scenarios as possible.

Looking at the other person will make him or her feel uncomfortable and this will make me feel more anxious. Alternatively, I may feel less anxious as I will not be focusing on myself. I have a memory from chidlhood when somebody asked me what I was staring at.

Carry out new behaviour and write down what actually happened here.

I found that I was actually much less anxious than I thought I would be. I did find myself shifting back to looking inwards a few times, but I noticed I was doing this and immediately started focusing externally once more. I found that overall I felt much more relaxed.

What did you learn from this process?
How likely are you to carry out this new behaviour again?

It was much easier than I thought. I felt much more relaxed. I am going to do this as much as possible going forwards now.

Behavioural experiment sheet

Describe old behaviour or safety behaviour

Describe new behaviour

How will you carry out new behaviour?

Predictions about what will happen when you drop the safety behaviour. Write down as many scenarios as possible.

Carry out new behaviour and write down what actually happened here.

What did you learn from this process?
How likely are you to carry out this new behaviour again?

Potential behavioural experiments for social anxiety

SAFETY BEHAVIOUR	NEW ALTERNATIVE BEHAVIOUR
Go to the toilet before going out (related to fear of using lavatories and others overhearing lavatory use). Not being able to urinate at a urinal.	Use a lavatory in a public building. Use the lavatory while others are there. If male, urinate in a urinal while other men are there. If unable to urinate, wait for as long as is necessary.
Have someone with you when going to social situations.	Go to a social event alone.
Carry a bottle of water (to help with a dry mouth).	Leave water at home. Let dry mouth be there.
Drink alcohol before going out to relax.	Go to social events in a state of sobriety.
Hold onto or lean onto something supportive to hide shaking or trembling.	Allow hands to tremble. Allow others to see. Use external focus to assess what actually happens.
Sit close to an exit, so as to escape unnoticed.	Sit in a central area where you will have to move past people to leave the situation.
Wear light clothing, fan self, or stand near a window or a doorway to prevent over-heating. Alternatively, wear more clothes to conceal sweating.	Wear normal clothing and stand in a warmer part of the room. Use external focus to assess what actually happens.
Have tissue ready to wipe hands to conceal sweaty hands.	Shake hands with somebody without wiping your hands first with tissues.
Use heavy make-up to avoid others noticing blushing or cover face with hair.	Use less make-up. Give permission for self to blush. Allow blushing experience to come and go. Use external focus to assess what actually happens.
Drink out of a bottle rather than a glass to avoid others noticing shaking hands.	Drink out of a glass. If hands shake, give permission for this to occur. Focus externally to assess what actually happens.
Have stories ready to put on an act of social competence and to have something interesting to say.	Go through a social event without telling stories or offering an acting performance. Practise active listening instead, using external focus.
Focus on self to assess social performance.	Focus on others. Be really curious and interested about what others think and how they behave.
Avoid conversations with people.	Start a conversation with a new person. Introduce yourself to them by telling them your name.
Stand in a corner to keep a low profile.	Stand in a more prominent position where you are likely to interact with more people.

Potential behavioural experiments for social anxiety (continued)

SAFETY BEHAVIOUR	NEW ALTERNATIVE BEHAVIOUR
Keep conversations as short as possible to avoid revealing anything that could be self-incriminating.	Offer up some information about yourself that you would not normally. Assess what others' reactions are.
Focus on appearance.	Focus on what you like about other people's appearance.
Try to control facial expressions by focusing on face.	Focus externally and give permission for your face to do whatever it chooses.
Avoid eye contact with others.	Increase eye contact with others.
Mentally rehearse what is being said before it is said.	Speak without thinking and assess what actually happens.
Have excuses about why you need to leave pre-planned and ready.	Go to events without any pre-planning.

Potential behavioural experiments for anxiety and panic attacks

SAFETY BEHAVIOUR	NEW ALTERNATIVE BEHAVIOUR
Carry a supply of diazepam everywhere.	Leave diazepam in the car when you visit the shops.
Do not move too fast for fear of heart rate increase.	Increase heart rate and observe what actually happens.
Drink alcohol before going out to relax.	Drink alcohol after you go out.
Avoid situations where you have had panic attacks in the past.	Gradually approach situations where panic attacks have occurred before.
Do not eat before going out (if you have a fear of vomiting).	Eat a small meal before going out.
Go to the rest room before going out (if fear is related to loss of control of bowels).	Hold off going to the rest room before going out unless you really need to go.
Have a safe person with you.	Leave safe person for a little while and see how you cope.
Carry a brown paper bag to breathe in and out of.	Leave brown paper bag at home.
Carry a bottle of water just in case of dry mouth.	Hydrate with water before you go out.
Carry a plastic bag if fear is related to vomiting.	Leave plastic bag at home for longer period.
Sit near to an exit.	Gradually sit further and further from an exit.
Hold onto or lean onto something supportive.	Trust your body's ability to balance without holding onto anything.
Hold breath.	Focus on breathing.
Monitor anxiety.	Focus externally.
Fan self to stop self over-heating.	Give permission for body to heat up as much as it wants.
Distract self to avoid noticing emotion.	Focus on emotion, stay with it, and take it with you.

Potential behavioural experiments for health anxiety

SAFETY BEHAVIOUR	NEW ALTERNATIVE BEHAVIOUR
Monitor any unusual symptoms in body.	Focus externally.
Seek reassurance from loved ones.	Hold off seeking reassurance.
Make an appointment with doctor.	Limit appointments with doctor. Make appointment as far ahead as possible.
Go onto the internet to complete research.	Limit internet searches or postpone them.
Complete online health assessments to self-diagnose.	Watch television instead or read a book.
Worry about ability to cope with various disorders.	Decide to deal with eventualities if or when they happen.
Request repeated medical tests from doctor.	Limit tests to reasonable intervals discussed with your doctor.
Request medical tests to rule out disorders when there are no symptoms.	Wait for symptoms before requesting a medical test.
Avoid doctors completely.	Approach doctor if feeling unwell.

Potential behavioural experiments for OCD

SAFETY BEHAVIOUR	NEW ALTERNATIVE BEHAVIOUR
Avoid situations or people that may trigger intrusive thoughts.	Carry out daily activities. Do not avoid people or places that you come across.
Retrace steps.	Postpone retracing steps.
Go back and check things that you are unsure of.	If you have checked once already, leave it.
Complete ritualistic behaviour, for example, touching wood.	Postpone ritualistic behaviour and wait for urge to die down.
Complete mental calculations in head to distract from emotions.	Put 100% attention onto feeling feelings.
Push away intrusive thoughts if you believe that thinking about them will make them real.	Recognise intrusive thoughts. Allow them to come and go in their own time.
Complete activities a certain number of times.	Reduce the number of times that you complete activities.
Perform activities in a particular order.	Deliberately change the order.
Wear particular make-up or jewellery.	Change make-up or jewellery.
Carry certain items.	Leave items behind for gradually longer periods of time.
Check and re-check that you have not left anything behind.	Check once and go.
Look for reassurance from others.	Drop reassurance.
Encourage others to engage in checks or rituals.	If you need to complete a checking behaviour, do it on your own. Ask relatives not to cooperate with completing obsessional behaviours.
Stay with safe people.	Spend time away from safe people.
Clean things to avoid contamination.	Reduce cleaning activity. Postpone cleaning.
Hold on to items or hoard things.	Gradually throw away things that you don't need any more. Throw away at least one piece of clutter a day.

Potential behavioural experiments for phobic anxiety

SAFETY BEHAVIOUR	NEW ALTERNATIVE BEHAVIOUR
Avoid particular objects or places.	Gradually expose self to certain objects and places.
Avoid certain forms of transport.	Gradually approach transport. For example, enter stationary train. Get on and off. Work your way towards making a very small trip.
Take specific routes to avoid certain things such as bridges or motorways.	Change route to approach feared things. For example, make a short journey on a quiet motorway, or travel across a small bridge.
Avoid certain tastes, smells, sensations, or feelings that might produce anxiety.	Gradually learn to tolerate certain physical or sensory experiences.
Ask for reassurance or others to check things for you.	Avoid asking for reassurance and if you need to check something do it yourself.
Avoid watching television about certain feared subjects.	Watch programmes about certain feared subjects. Make room for your feelings while you do this.
Try to be in control of others. For example, if phobic of travel, trying to give advice to the driver about how to drive safely.	Allow others to drive.

Desensitising yourself to changing completing behaviour

To desensitise yourself to changing your behaviour you will need to note down all of the a) situations that you have been avoiding and b) safety behaviours that you currently fear dropping. You will then need to grade each item on your list in terms of the level of anxiety you will experience when either approaching a feared situation or dropping a safety behaviour. Rate the most frightening item on your list as a 10 and then compare every other situation to it, giving each item on your list an anxiety score out of 10. Paul's list is shown on page 122. The situation that provoked the most anxiety for Paul was going on an aeroplane, so Paul recorded his anxiety level with this behaviour as a 10. Every other item on Paul's list was compared against this.

Once you have completed your list, you will then need to work your way through it starting with the behaviours that provoke the lowest level of anxiety. It is very important for any behaviour that you change on your list that you accept your feelings while doing it (see Chapter 10). You will also need to be mindful when completing items on your list that you do this without using any additional safety behaviours, such as holding your breath, distracting yourself, etc. Do not move onto higher anxiety evoking situations on your list until your anxiety about completing things lower down on your list has reduced significantly or is easily tolerated.

If you find that your anxiety does not reduce, don't persist with this approach. It might be that there are earlier emotionally unprocessed memories or traumatic experiences that need attention or working through. Unprocessed memories or traumas can often be a contributory factor to anticipatory anxiety in the present time mode. If this is the case, we recommend that you don't try to work on these memories on your own. You will be better off working with a trained therapist.

Paul's experience

One item on Paul's list was attending his psychology sessions without his partner. The first time that Paul left to attend his psychology session on his own his anxiety rose to quite a high level. He was able to make room for his feelings, giving permission for himself to feel anxious while carrying out this new behaviour. As you might imagine after Paul attended his psychology session alone for the first time the primitive part of his brain discovered that nothing actually happened and it altered the threat level for him attending future appointments alone. Following this, Paul's anxiety about attending appointments by himself reduced significantly and he attended all of his future appointments alone. Paul also reported that other items on his list seemed far more achievable than he previously thought and they did not create as much anxiety as he initially anticipated. As he progressed through his list Paul noted that in general terms his mood had improved and that he had felt more confident.

Please note that each individual fear can be broken down into much smaller units. For example, going on a tube could be broken down into numerous small challenges (see Table 10). Each of these challenges can be further broken down into even smaller challenges (see Table 11), and so on.

Paul's list:

- Make room for and accept feelings when feeling slightly anxious. (1)
- Attend psychology appointment without partner. (3)
- In session raise heart rate by completing gentle exercise. (5)
- Tell a friend about my panic attacks. (5.5)
- In session breathe out rapidly to expel carbon dioxide which leads to dizzy feeling in the head. Do I faint? (6)
- Do not use anti-anxiety medication before carrying out anxiety-evoking activities. (7)
- Do not carry anti-anxiety medication just in case. (7.5)
- Deliberately sit in the middle of a row of seats in a cinema/theatre. (8)
- Don't go to the toilet just before I go out (related to fear of losing control of bowels). (8)
- Be a passenger in a car rather than the driver (short trip non-motorway). (8.5)
- Drive on a motorway rather than a country road (short trip). (9)
- Drive on motorway (long trip). (9.5)
- Passenger in an uncrowded tube (related to fear of losing control). (9.5)
- Passenger in a crowded tube (underground railway). (10)
- Passenger in an aeroplane (short haul). (10)

Table 10. Example of a systematic desensitisation sheet

Systematic desensitisation sheet

Overall target situation, object, or behaviour for desensitisation
Travelling on a tube (underground railway).

Individual area for desensitisation	Predicted distress level 0 to 10
Go into foyer of tube station. Stay there until distress reduces to zero and then exit tube station.	2
Go down long escalator and back up to surface again.	3
Use lift.	6
Go on overland train accompanied by someone.	7
Go on overland train alone.	8
Go on tube accompanied by therapist.	8
Go on tube accompanied by friend.	9
Go on tube alone.	10

Table 11. Example of a systematic desensitisation sheet

Systematic desensitisation sheet

Overall target situation, object, or behaviour for desensitisation
Use lift (part of desensitisation process of going on a tube).

Individual area for desensitisation	Predicted distress level 0 to 10
Go to lift (not used much) with therapist.	1
Go in lift with doors open and get out again (with therapist).	2
Go in lift with doors open and get out again (without therapist).	3
Go in lift, let doors close and open, and get out again (with therapist).	4
Go in lift, let doors close and open and get out again (without therapist).	5
Go in lift, let doors close and open, go down or up one floor and get out again (with therapist).	5
Go in lift, let doors close and open, go down or up one floor and get out again (without therapist).	6
Go in lift, let doors close and open, go down or up two floors and get out again (without therapist).	6

Systematic desensitisation sheet

Overall target situation, object, or behaviour for desensitisation	

Individual area for desensitisation	Predicted distress level 0 to 10

Using exposure sheets

Exposure can be used as part of a process of desensitisation. When you use exposure you will need to stay in anxiety-provoking situations until your anxiety is very easy to tolerate. To assist with your learning process you could assess your anxiety level before, during, and after the situation you place yourself in or while you are using a new behaviour (we have placed Jenny's information in Table 12). After you have completed your exposure work, think about what you have learnt from your experience. This will further embed your experiential learning (learning by doing/experiencing).

Table 12. Jenny's exposure sheet

Exposure sheet

Time: Date:	Situation	Anxiety before (0 to 10 where 10 is max)	Anxiety during (0 to 10 where 10 is max)	Anxiety after (0 to 10 where 10 is max)	What did I learn?
7 pm 17 Jan	Staying with and welcoming anxiety during a social event	6	2	2	Staying with and welcoming anxiety during a social event

Exposure sheet

Time: Date:	Situation	Anxiety before (0 to 10 where 10 is max)	Anxiety during (0 to 10 where 10 is max)	Anxiety after (0 to 10 where 10 is max)	What did I learn?

CHAPTER 13

Conclusion

You have now come to the end of this book and hopefully you have a better understanding of your anxiety. You may also need to be aware that forming an improved relationship with your anxiety will involve you changing a) the way that you think, b) how you relate to your feelings, and c) how you behave. Changing the way that you think, feel, and behave is not as easy as it might seem, even if change is considered a good thing.

You are highly likely to meet resistance from yourself when you begin to approach change. But, when you can get past this resistance, you may learn new things from your new experiences, and you can use what you learn for the future – hopefully, even for the rest of your life. As humans, we have an inbuilt resistance to change. I'll explain what I mean using an example from science. Let's imagine that in the past a common view was that the world was flat. This fact 'the world is flat', was challenged by one scientist describing an alternative world view, in this case 'the world is round'. The scientist's new idea was supported by some evidence; for example, the horizon appeared to have a slight curvature. The scientist's new suggestions met resistance from the general population as certainty was replaced by uncertainty, or as the previously stable view of the world was challenged. Suggestions were put forward to test the new theory; for example, someone said, 'Let's organise a sailing expedition!' A man called Magellan volunteered to complete the expedition and he set off to circumnavigate the world. Uncertainty, unrest, resistance, and anxiety increased still further, as the challenge to the old world view became experiential. As we mentioned earlier, 'experiential' means that we are experiencing things directly for ourselves rather than simply thinking about them logically. The experiential phase of change is the most anxiety provoking for humans as it presents a position of not knowing. Potentially it is also one of the most frightening positions a thinking, or conceptualising, animal can find him-or herself in, and hence why we have such a built-in avoidance of it. Not knowing is associated with danger, and we are instinctively programmed to avoid what we perceive as dangerous.

Eventually, Magellan came back and the findings of his voyage were inspected, and the results measured. In this case, the crew from Magellan's expedition brought back items from the other side of the world, drew new revised maps, and reported that the world was not flat. The previous view of the world had begun to change. For a while there was still resistance. People disbelieved the evidence even though it was staring them in the face, and it was difficult for them to dispute it. However, after a period of time, uncertainty was gradually replaced by certainty and confidence in the new idea was reinforced. People's anxiety reduced and a period of reflection on the outcome followed. Eventually, the new world view was adopted by enough people, and it then became viewed as a fact. After a while the whole process started again, when another scientist suggested that the world was not round but a sphere flattened at its poles.

We are suggesting that your journey will follow a pattern in a predetermined order. A period of uncertainty will take place before change occurs. In this respect, as you approach the strategies that you will come across in this book, periods of experiential uncertainty will become a natural and arguably essential part of your learning process. If you decide to embrace your uncertainty about completing new exercises or new coping strategies, you will find that your uncertainty, like a chrysalis, will be used to transform you. Your period of uncertainty will pass and you will emerge from your old shell with increased confidence. Your distress will reduce and you will begin to reflect on the outcomes that you have achieved. The process will then begin again with the next new exercise that you try.

Another area that you will need to confront is habitual behaviour. Much of the time we can find ourselves falling into repetitive loops or habitual behaviours when we become highly emotional. (Habitual behaviours are behaviours that occur automatically.) Many of us use the same habitual behaviours over and over again to deal with our emotions in certain situations, even when we know that our strategies don't work. When we become distressed, states of high emotional arousal lead to primitive brain areas, located in the subcortical area, taking a central role. These primitive brain areas are governed by habitual behaviour, which tends to be automatic, inflexible, and rule-based. Habitual behaviour is generally thought to operate outside of conscious awareness and we revert to this quite strongly when under stress or when we are tired.

How to prevent relapse

In the earlier years of our practice, we noticed that after an average of about three to five years about 10% of clients returned to us with their original anxiety symptoms once more. These particular clients reported that after their period of treatment was complete they felt much happier and as a result didn't need to use the techniques they learnt as much. Over time, however, it seemed that our clients slowly forgot how to use them. As a result of this, over a period of years they gradually reverted back to their original position.

Working with these individuals for a second time usually involved just a few sessions, and generally much less treatment was required compared to when they initially came to us. They were able to quickly relearn the strategies that they used before and found it much easier to put change processes into place on their return to therapy. There was much less fear about using a process of accepting feelings and engaging in systematic desensitisation as these individuals were able to access useful evidence from their past experiences.

To reduce relapse problems with our clients, we began to use an idea that we referred to as the 'Law of Opposites' (Ridgeway & Manning, 2008). With this approach, at the end of treatment we would ask our clients to think about all the ideas that they might forget about or the behaviours that they could once again employ if they wanted to return to their original pre-therapy position. We encouraged our clients to make their list as exhaustive as possible. When our client's list was complete we asked them to think of solutions to each point on their list. Paul's list is shown in Table 13. The main aspect that Paul noticed on reflection was that he was more aware of his body's reactions to situations after therapy. Instead of interpreting signs of anxiety as an indication that something bad was going to happen to him, he now recognised that his body was creating a preparatory response. When he viewed his anxiety in this way he no longer felt as though anxiety was his enemy, and when he approached new situations he took his anxiety with him. Generally, he noticed that his anxiety only rose in the early stages, but as soon as he embraced it and he stayed in any particular situation it soon dissipated. A useful idea is to get your list out on a regular basis to assess if there is any slippage back to your previous way of approaching your symptoms. Keeping a log that documents your journey with anxiety may also prove useful. Later on, if you need to, you can quickly revise or recap any approaches that worked for you.

Best of luck with your CBT.

Table 13. An example of the law of opposites

Previous approach	New approach
Avoid uncomfortable feelings.	Approach uncomfortable feelings.
Distract self: keep mind off things.	Focus on feelings.
Perceive anxiety symptoms as threatening. Try to escape from them.	Perceive anxiety as a part of the body that is trying to help me. Embrace symptoms.
Control anxiety. Try to extinguish symptoms as soon as possible.	Allow emotions to be in my body for as long as they need to be there.
Worry about potential problems that may occur so that solutions can be applied.	Drop pre-planning before going into situations that are associated with panic symptoms.
Use safety behaviours, such as using country roads, pre-driving routes.	Drop safety behaviours. If I notice that I am using avoidance, approach problems instead.

Previous approach	New approach

References and additional reading

Arnsten, A., Raskind, M., Taylor, F. & Connor, D. (2015) The effects of stress exposure on prefrontal cortex: Translating basic research into successful treatments for post-traumatic stress disorder. Neurobiology of Stress, pp. 89–99.

Bandura, A. (1977) Social Learning Theory. Prentice-Hall.

Beck, J. (2011) Cognitive Behavior Therapy: Second Edition – Basics and Beyond. The Guildford Press.

Butler, G. (2009). Overcoming Social Anxiety & Shyness. Robinson.

Cabral, R. & Nardi E. (2012) Anxiety and inhibition of panic attacks within translational and prospective research contexts. Trends in Psychiatry.

Clark, D.M. (1986) A cognitive approach to panic. Behaviour Research and Therapy, 24: 461–470.

Clark, D.M. & Wells, A. (1995) A cognitive model of social phobia. In Social Phobia – Diagnosis, Assessment, and Treatment (eds. R.G. Heimberg, M.R. Liebowitz, D. Hope et al.), pp. 69–93. New York: Guilford.

Debiec, J. & Sullivan, R. (2014) Intergenerational transmission of emotional trauma through amygdala-dependent mother-to-infant transfer of specific fear. Proceedings of the National Academy of Sciences, DOI: 10.1073/pnas.1316740111.

Golman, D. (1996) Emotional Intelligence: Why It Can Matter More Than IQ. Bloomsbury.

Greenberger, D. & Padesky, C. (1995) Mind Over Mood: Change How You Feel by Changing the Way That You Think. Guildford Press.

Guzmán, Y., Tronson, N., Jovasevic, K., Sato, K., Guedea, A., Mizukami, H., Nishimori, K. & Radulovic. J. (2013) Fear-enhancing effects of septal oxytocin receptors. Nature Neuroscience,DOI: 10.1038/nn.3465.

Kennerley, H. (2009) Overcoming Anxiety: A Self-Help Guide Using Cognitive Behavioural Techniques. Robinson.

Kinman, G. & Grant, L. (2010) Exploring stress resilience in trainee social workers: The role of emotional and social competencies. British Journal of Social Work, 10.1093/bjsw/bcq088.

Krusemark, E. & Li, W. (2012) Enhanced olfactory sensory perception of threat in anxiety: An event-related fMRI study. Chemosensory Perception, 5(1): 37 DOI: 10.1007/s12078-011-9111-7.

LeDoux, J.E., Iwata, J., Cicchetti, P., & Reis, D.J. (1988) Different projections of the central amygdaloid nucleus mediate autonomic and behavioral correlates of conditioned fear. Journal of Neuroscience, Jul;8(7): 2517–29.

Logue, M.W., Bauver, S.R., Kremen, W.S., Franz, C.E., Eisen, S.A., Tsuang, M.T., Grant, M.D. & Lyons, M.J. (2011) Evidence of overlapping genetic diathesis of panic attacks and gastrointestinal disorders in a sample of male twin pairs. Twin Research and Human Genetics, Feb; 14(1): 16–24. doi: 10.1375/twin.14.1.16.

McIlrath, D. & Huitt, W. The teaching-learning process: A discussion of models. Educational Psychology Interactive. Valdosta, GA: Valdosta State University. Retrieved 2016 from http://www.edpsycinteractive.org/papers/modeltch.html.

Moorey, S. (2010) The six cycles maintenance model: Growing a 'vicious flower' for depression. Behaviour and Cognitive Psychotherapy, Mar; 38(2): 173–84.

Moulding, R., Coles, M.E., Abramowitz, J.S., Alcolado, G.M., Alonso, P., Belloch, A., Bouvard, M., Clark, D.A., Doron, G., Fernández-Álvarez, H., García-Soriano, G., Ghisi, M., Gómez, B., Inozu, M., Radomsky, A.S., Shams, G., Sica, C., Simos, G. & Wong, W. (2014) Part 2. They scare because we care: the relationship between obsessive intrusive thoughts and appraisals and control strategies across 15 cities. Journal of Obsessive-Compulsive and Related Disorders, 3(3): 280–291.

Rachman, S., Coughtrey, S.R. & Radomsky, A. (2015) The Oxford Guide to the Treatment of Mental Contamination. The Oxford University Press.

Ridgeway, N., & Manning, J. (2008). Think about your thinking: To stop depression. Foulsham & Co.

Seger, C.A. (2011) A critical review of habit learning and the basal ganglia. Frontiers in Systems Neuroscience, Aug 30; 5:66.

Teachman, B., Marker, C. & Clerkin, E. (2010) Catastrophic misinterpretations as a predictor of symptom change during treatment for panic disorder. Journal of Consulting and Clinical Psychology, 78(6): 964–973.

Veale, D. & Wilson, R. (2005) Overcoming Obsessive Compulsive Disorder: A Self-help Guide using Cognitive Behavioral Techniques. Constable & Robinson Ltd.

Wells, A. (1997) Cognitive Therapy of Anxiety Disorders: A Practice Manual and Conceptual Guide. Wiley.

Wilson, R. & Veale, D. (2009) Overcoming Health Anxiety. Robinson.

Glossary

Abdominal breathing: Process of breathing that involves relaxing the abdomen and taking in air to the bottom of the lungs.

Amygdala: Small area of brain tissue within the limbic system, responsible for activating the body's fight-flight-or-freeze response.

Anxiety: An emotion that is experienced when the body is moving into a prepared state to deal with a potential threat.

Automatic responses: Responses that occur automatically/outside of conscious awareness.

Behavioural strategies: Making an adjustment to your behaviour and monitoring the impact of resulting changes.

Catastrophic misinterpretation: A frightening and exaggerated thought connected to magnification of perceived stimuli.

Catecholamines: Chemical messengers used by cells to communicate with one another.

Cognitive distortions: Thinking patterns that distort perception of reality.

Cognitive interventions: Strategies based on changing mental reactions.

Cognitive models: Ways of explaining how psychological distress is maintained.

Conditioned response: A response that occurs automatically as a result of repeated actions towards particular stimuli.

Coping strategies: Strategies that have been of some assistance in reducing distress.Core beliefs: Strongly held beliefs about the self.

Counter-intuitive: Ideas that we would not naturally gravitate towards.

Default response: An automatic response based on previous experiences and past conditioning.

Desensitising: Gradually being able to tolerate a feeling by staying in a situation until the feeling feels more bearable.

Diazepam: A medication often prescribed as a muscle relaxant.

Dissociation: A mental and physical state where an individual feels a loss of connection with his or her body.

Distraction: A process that individuals use to avoid experiencing painful emotions.

Emotional reference point: A mechanism used by babies who look towards caregivers to determine how they might react at an emotional level.

Experiential: A process of experiencing through the senses.

External focus: Placing one's attention onto one's external environment.

Habitual behaviours: Behaviours that we are inclined to use because we have used them so many times before.

Holistic: Multiple processes connected together working in parallel.

Hyperventilation: A process of rapid shallow breathing where an individual breathes out too much carbon dioxide.Hypothesis: An idea based on scientific theory.

Intrusive thoughts: Thoughts that enter awareness uninvited. These thoughts are usually accompanied by heightened emotion.

Mindfulness: A process of staying in the present moment, bringing conscious awareness back to the present, and deliberately moving away from thoughts about the past or the future.

Mood regulation: An ability to have some management of one's feelings.

Negative automatic thoughts: Thoughts in the background of the mind that have the potential to keep individuals emotionally distressed.

Negative reinforcement: A process of repeated behaviour in which negative emotion is reduced leading to greater likelihood of the same future behaviour.

Neocortex: Highly developed area of the mind responsible for logical, rational, and analytical thinking.

Phobic response: An automatic response associated with heightened anxiety, connected to a specific trigger or cue.

Plasticity: The brain's ability to repair itself and grow the more that it is used.

Prefrontal cortex: An area of the brain that acts as a relay between the subcortical regions of the brain and the neocortex. It is also responsible for dampening emotional reactions and quietening the mind.

Registered therapists: Registered therapists are members of professional bodies. Professional bodies are organisations that check out their therapists to make sure that they have the required training to do their jobs properly.

Rumination: A cognitive process that involves churning of thoughts connected to the self in the past over and over in the mind.

Safety behaviours: Behaviours utilised to reduce emotional distress in the short term.

Self-fulfilling prophecy: When something occurs despite your very best attempts to prevent that particular thing occurring.

Self-perpetuating: A situation that is kept in place through its own actions.

Serotonin: A chemical messenger, serotonin plays a huge part in the body's overall physical and mental functioning.

Subcortical regions: Brain areas located in the lower half of the brain.

Suppressing emotions: An act of pushing down painful or upsetting feelings.

Threat perception centre: An area within the brain responsible for noticing stimuli associated with past fear or trauma.

Traumatic incidents: Events that have occurred in the past connected to highly distressing emotions.

Unprocessed memory: An experience that the mind has not fully dealt with.

Vicarious trauma: When people develop trauma responses as a result of observing other people's intense emotional reactions.

Common medications

Alprazolam: A benzodiazepine prescribed for panic, generalised anxiety, phobias, social anxiety, OCD

Amitriptyline: A tricyclic antidepressant

Atenolol: A beta-blocker prescribed for anxiety

Buspirone: A mild tranquilliser prescribed for generalised anxiety, OCD and panic

Chlordiazepoxide: A benzodiazepine prescribed for generalised anxiety, phobias

Citalopram: A selective serotonin reuptake inhibitor commonly prescribed for mixed anxiety and depression

Clomipramine: A tricyclic antidepressant

Clonazepam: A benzodiazepine prescribed for panic, generalised anxiety, phobias, social anxiety

Desipramine: A tricyclic antidepressant

Diazepam: A benzodiazepine prescribed for generalised anxiety, panic, phobias

Doxepin: A tricyclic antidepressant

Duloxetine: A serotonin-norepinephrine reuptake inhibitor

Escitalopram Oxalate: A selective serotonin reuptake inhibitor

Fluoxetine: A selective serotonin reuptake inhibitor

Fluvoxamine: A selective serotonin reuptake inhibitor

Gabapentin: An anticonvulsant prescribed for generalised anxiety and social anxiety

Imipramine: A tricyclic antidepressant

Lorazepam: A benzodiazepine prescribed for generalised anxiety, panic, phobias

Nortriptyline: A tricyclic antidepressant

Oxazepam: A benzodiazepine prescribed for generalised anxiety, phobias

Paroxetine: A selective serotonin reuptake inhibitor

Phenelzine: A monoamine oxidase inhibitor

Pregabalin: An anticonvulsant prescribed for generalised anxiety disorder

Propanalol: A beta blocker prescribed for anxiety

Sertraline: A selective serotonin reuptake inhibitor

Tranylcypromine: A monoamine oxidase inhibitor

Valproate: An anticonvulsant prescribed for panic

Venlafaxine: A serotonin-norepinephrine reuptake inhibitor

Index

A counter-intuitive solution to anxiety, 96
Abdominal breathing, 100
Accepting feelings, 97, 130
Alcohol, 13, 14, 103, 115, 117
Avoidance, 11, 13, 95, 100, 110, 128
Basal ganglia, 99, 134, 148
Behavioural experiments, 109
Brain organisation, 5
Breaking cycles, 69
caffeine, 103
Catecholamines, 7, 135
CBT, 89, 90, 91, 92, 93, 97, 99
CBT cycles, 37, 63
Challenging NATs, 76
Cognitive distortions, 24, 135
Cold showers, 103
Counter-intuitive, 96
Critical incidents, 39
Depression, 6, 134, 137, 148
Diaries, 18
Downward arrow exercise, 34, 35
EMDR, 102, 103
Experiential, 18, 19, 109, 126
Exposure, 126, 133, 147
Feeling mind, 5
Focused detachment, 20
Focused distraction, 101, 102
Generic CBT cycle, the, 45
Guided imagery, 101
Habitual behaviour, 129
Health anxiety, 15, 53, 118
Intrusive thoughts, 89, 92, 93, 136
Law of Opposites, 130
Librarian, the, 91, 92
Limiting beliefs, 34
Magellan, 128, 129
Massage, 102
Medication, 101, 102, 122, 135
Mindfulness, 102, 136
NATs, 45, 73, 76, 77, 83
Negative reinforcement, 11, 12
Observation, 18, 20, 43, 102
OCD, 57, 59, 60, 74, 75, 119, 137
OCD cycles, 57
Panic, 117, 133, 134, 137, 147, 148
Phobic anxiety, 16
Post-trauma symptoms, 16
Prefrontal cortex, 6, 18, 63, 97, 101, 102, 133, 147
Relapse, 129, 130
Research, 93, 103, 133, 147

Rules, 28, 29, 34, 37, 38, 39, 40, 41, 49, 50, 53, 54, 57, 58, 63, 64, 69
Rumination, 89, 102, 136
Safe place exercise, 104, 105
Safety behaviours, 11, 13, 34, 37, 39, 49, 53, 95, 115, 116, 117, 118, 119, 120, 121
Self-focus, 49
Self-monitoring, 49, 110
Self-phobic model, 67
Self-phobic response, 67
Self-reflection, 20
Social anxiety, 13, 49, 50, 51, 74, 76, 77, 110, 115, 116, 137
Subcortical, 97, 99, 102, 129
Subcortical region, 5, 99
Systematic desensitisation, 123, 124, 130
Systematic relaxation, 101
Thinking mind, the, 5, 7, 8, 10
Traditional CBT cycle, the, 43
Thought challenging records, 77, 81
Worry, 9, 11, 53, 89, 92, 93, 97, 102

Made in the USA
Middletown, DE
27 December 2017